RISK
ALL THAT MATTERS

About the authors

Clive Steeper is an expert in understanding and managing risk in business. He has led several international businesses with responsibility for managing risk in relation to the introduction of new technologies into the global marketplace. Now an executive coach, consultant and facilitator, Clive works with all types of organization.

In addition, Clive has been a team manager for an International Motorsport Team, as well as a tyre engineer and motorsport instructor, where managing risk is critical. He delivers lectures around the world on the subject of risk in business, and currently challenges himself as a racing driver.

Sue Stockdale is a motivational speaker, executive coach and record-breaking explorer. She works with some of Europe's top companies to improve their leadership and team-working capabilities. Her academic background includes an MBA in Entrepreneurship and a Masters degree in Quality Management. Sue speaks regularly to multinational corporations, academic institutions and small businesses on the subject of risk-taking.

As a risk-taker herself, Sue was the first British woman to ski to the Magnetic North Pole, and she has been on expeditions to Antarctica, Greenland and the Geographical North Pole.

Clive Steeper and Sue Stockdale are also co-authors of *Motivating People, Cope with Change at Work* and *The Personality Workbook*.

RISK

Clive Steeper and
Sue Stockdale

First published in Great Britain in 2015 by John Murray Learning. An Hachette UK company.

First published in US in 2015 by The McGraw-Hill Companies, Inc.

This edition published in 2015 by John Murray Learning

British Library Cataloguing in Publication Data: a catalogue record for this title is available from the British Library.

Library of Congress Catalog Card Number: on file.

Paperback ISBN 978 1 473 60247 2

eBook ISBN 978 1 473 60249 6

1

The publisher has used its best endeavours to ensure that any website addresses referred to in this book are correct and active at the time of going to press. However, the publisher and the author have no responsibility for the websites and can make no guarantee that a site will remain live or that the content will remain relevant, decent or appropriate.

The publisher has made every effort to mark as such all words which it believes to be trademarks. The publisher should also like to make it clear that the presence of a word in the book, whether marked or unmarked, in no way affects its legal status as a trademark.

Every reasonable effort has been made by the publisher to trace the copyright holders of material in this book. Any errors or omissions should be notified in writing to the publisher, who will endeavour to rectify the situation for any reprints and future editions.

Typeset by Cenveo® Publisher Services.

Printed and bound in Great Britain by CPI Group (UK) Ltd, Croydon CR0 4YY.

John Murray Learning policy is to use papers that are natural, renewable and recyclable products and made from wood grown in sustainable forests. The logging and manufacturing processes are expected to conform to the environmental regulations of the country of origin.

John Murray Learning
338 Euston Road
London NW1 3BH
www.hodder.co.uk

**Also available
in ebook**

Contents

Foreword

This book is an integration of our knowledge and experience of risk-taking throughout our lives, from both the practical and the theoretical perspective. From the icy wastes of the Arctic to the engine roar and tyre screeching at the race circuit to business deals and health, we have both understood the implications of analysing risks and making decisions in potentially life-and-death situations. We hope that this book will give readers a new insight into risk and how it affects their lives, and inspire them to practise their risk-taking.

Chapter 1 offers some definitions of risk and explores how we can assess and manage risk in our daily lives. Chapter 2 will provide greater insight into understanding our propensity for risk, and the impact of personality on how we view risk. Chapter 3 will take the broader perspective and consider to what degree society is becoming more risk-averse. Chapter 4 considers risk in the business world and explores issues such as reputational risk, trust, compliance risk and financial risk. Chapter 5 provides some practical examples of how risk is managed by individuals and in businesses. Finally, Chapter 6 focuses on the future, and how the issue of risk is linked to changes in technology, the environment, society, demographics and global concerns such as economic instability and health.

www.clivesteeper.com

www.suestockdale.com

Acknowledgements

Thank you to everyone who has contributed to this book with their insights and their support, in particular Caspar Berry, David Brabham, Dr Rebecca Harding, Charlotte Howard, Sarah Kuijlaars, Professor Hugh Montgomery, Dr Martyn Newman, Grant Phillips, Professor Chris Rapley CBE, Tony Rose and Dr Geoff Trickey.

1

What is risk?

'[Risk is] the probability that a particular adverse event occurs during a stated period of time, or results from a particular challenge.'

Royal Society for the Prevention of Accidents,
Risk Assessment: A Study Group report *(1983)*

'[Risk is] the combination of the probability of an event and its consequence. Consequences can range from positive to negative.'

Institute of Risk Management

Some say that risk is all around us. Is it, or is it just a human invention? There is no one single universal definition of risk, yet the word 'risk' is commonly used in the English language. The word derives from the early Italian *risicare*, which means 'to dare'. In this sense, risk is a choice rather than a fate.

Two definitions of risk are given on the opening page of this chapter. Another definition is that it is 'a systematic way of dealing with hazards and insecurities and introduced by modernization itself' (Beck, 1992). A further alternative definition is that it is 'the combined answers to (1) What can go wrong? (2) How likely is it? and (3) What are the consequences?' (US Nuclear Regulatory Commission).

No matter which definition of risk you subscribe to, it is fair to say that risk is a phenomenon created by the human mind. It is based on what we see, hear and are told about by others; and it is our own interpretation of these factors that will determine how we react to risk. For example, some view skydiving as a fun pursuit, while for others it is a risk too far.

The media can also play a major role in shaping our perceptions of risk. Often the focus is on the perceived risks rather than the benefits of a course of action and, while this can be helpful at times, the media can also have too influential a role in driving the government response to risk issues. Some recent examples in the UK include the BSE crisis and health and safety policy in schools.

It is not uncommon to find the word 'hazard' used in conjunction with danger or risk. This perhaps helps to explain why the terms are often interchangeable when we are considering health and safety. A hazard is often thought of as a potential source of injury or harm or as having an adverse health effect on something or someone under particular conditions.

Encapsulating one definition of risk is difficult and it is made more complex when the word 'risk' is included in such phrases as:

▶ **risk management** – 'the identification, assessment and prioritization of risks followed by the co-ordinated and economical application of resources to minimize, monitor, and control the probability and/or impact of unfortunate events, or to maximize the realization of opportunities' (Douglas Hubbard in Hubbard, 2009).

▶ **risk assessment** – 'the determination of quantitative or qualitative value of risk related to a concrete situation and a recognized threat or hazard' (Wikipedia).

▶ Assessing risk

We tend to assess risk based on:

▶ our perception of the number of options we have

▶ the outcomes we value

▶ what we believe will happen if we choose a particular course of action.

For example, it can be as simple as thinking about what might happen if you eat a carton of yoghurt after its use-by date, or cycle in a busy environment without a helmet.

4

▲ How do we judge risk?

With increasing amounts of information now in the public domain, it is little wonder that people have a greater awareness of risk in everyday life. This information can come from a variety of sources, and it includes opinions as well as facts. However, the accuracy or bias of the information can be difficult to discern. Therefore we need to be able to judge the relevance and credibility of the information sources before we can decide on the probability of a potential outcome. That may be more challenging for someone who has had limited experience of taking risks.

For example, according to a Forbes article in 2008, the most hazardous sport in the USA is basketball, with over half a million injuries every year. Would this information make you more or less likely to play basketball? In order to assess potential risks, we need to consider further questions in relation to this information and the way it is presented. The Forbes article does not provide details about the various types of injury, the level and speed of recovery for the individuals, or whether there were lasting effects. The table below shows the ten most hazardous sports from the Forbes article:

▼ The ten most hazardous sports in the US, 2008

Position	Sport	Annual estimated number of injuries
1	Basketball	529,837
2	Cycling	490,434
3	American football	460,210
4	ATVs – all-terrain vehicles, mopeds, mini-bikes	275,123
5	Baseball, softball	274,867
6	Exercise, exercise equipment	269,249
7	Soccer	186,544
8	Swimming	164,607
9	Skiing, snowboarding	96,119
10	Lacrosse, rugby, miscellaneous ball games	85,580

Source: *Forbes* magazine, 29 May 2008

From the list, we might get the impression that basketball, cycling and American football offer the highest risk of injury. But is this true? For the answer, we need to consider a broader context.

Our personal experiences also influence our approach to risk. Having read the list above, you may recall an example of a sports injury you had or that you heard that someone else had incurred. This is known as **availability bias**, a term first coined by Amos Tversky and Daniel Kahneman (1973), and it explains how our intuitive estimate of risk is constructed from a biased sample of the experiences we have had that come readily to mind.

We also use rational thinking to assess risk. Continuing with the sports injuries example, we might choose to rationally assess the number of participants in each sport versus the number of injuries. The answer could help us get a different perspective on the information provided.

With further analysis, we could also consider the impact of age profile on the data, as it might be assumed that the older participants who have not maintained their level of fitness are more likely to have injuries. Also, if the list included professional or semi-professional players, that population – compared to the amateur players – could also skew the assessment of risk.

None of this discussion is intended to suggest that the information given in the Forbes article is wrong, inaccurate or misleading. Instead, it is used to demonstrate that perspectives on risk can be influenced. Therefore it is important to consider risk from a variety of perspectives rather than automatically taking things at face value, or avoiding risk based only on the initial data you read.

▶ Factors used to assess risk

By now, you may have begun to recognize that there is more to risk than you originally thought. Referring back to the Forbes data, if you had begun with the goal of participating in a sport that minimizes the chance of being injured, you may have used the following to assess the risks:

- The available options (basketball, cycling, rugby, skiing, soccer, etc.)

- The outcomes you value (enjoyment, pleasure, maintaining a healthy body)

- Beliefs about what might follow if you choose each option (if I go skiing, I might break my leg).

If you made your decision using only the data provided, it may have led you to play a ball game or go skiing, as those sports show comparatively fewer injuries than basketball or cycling. Yet if you asked an insurance company which sport they assess as more likely to cause injury, it is likely that they would put skiing further up the list because they may use a different method of evaluating risk to make their decision. Assessing and managing risk is really down to the individual depending on a combination of logic, emotion, external information and previous experience to make their decision.

Personality is an important factor that influences our attitude to risk. Over the last few years, some interesting work has been conducted by Psychological Consultancy Ltd (PCL) to measure an individual's propensity for risk. Out of this research a model was developed, highlighting eight risk types. It shows that an individual's attitude to risk is heavily influenced by their personality traits, which can range from prudent and wary to spontaneous and adventurous (see Chapter 2).

▶ The benefits of risk-taking

When we think about risk, it is rarely given a balanced viewpoint, and often the focus is on the downside, not the potential upside or benefits of risk-taking. However, in order for society and human beings to progress, it is vital that we do take risks. Improvement, and even excellence, is something people may strive for, and if we learn from high achievers, we can understand that taking risks is an essential part of human performance improvement.

Think in terms of advances in science, new product development, technology, alternative energy, sustainable transport, capital to support new business ventures and many other areas of society. No new ideas can be furthered without someone taking a risk. The benefit to a venture capitalist of investing in a start-up is the potential of a healthy financial return. However, most venture capitalists would recognize that well over 50 per cent of their investments are unlikely to exceed their growth expectations. Instead, they hope that, among the companies they select, there will be an equivalent of the next Google or Facebook that will deliver greater financial returns.

At an individual level, it is beneficial to take risks on a regular basis. While these activities may seem inconsequential, for the person taking the risk they may seem massive. For example, daring to say 'I love you' to your partner and hoping that they respond positively can be extremely risky for some. Having a meeting with your manager to tell them that you want a pay rise may feel risky to another. What these small acts do is provide practice in risk-taking, and the more humans are able to practise coping with risk, success and failure, the better they will be placed to deal with uncertainty, disappointment and success in the future.

Taking risks also makes us feel good. This is because taking part in challenging or risky activities triggers the release of dopamine, a feel-good neurotransmitter that is part of the brain's reward system. These issues are explored in more detail in Chapter 2.

▶ Risk and uncertainty

Uncertainty is also relevant to an exploration of risk. In the examples above, the entrepreneur cannot be certain that the new business venture will be a success, and the investor is not certain of a good return on their investment; yet they are prepared to act in the face of uncertainty in order to gain something that they perceive is of value.

To reduce uncertainty, many large companies use quantitative data to provide greater insight. Rebecca Harding, CEO at Delta Economics in London and former Chief Economist at The Work Foundation, explains that her company fulfils this need by providing quantitative forecasts on trade, economic growth and trade finance, to help businesses make decisions. 'As a result', she says, 'organizations are able to quantify uncertainty as a measure of risk, which can then be insured against.'

Think about a government or a large institution that is looking to embark on a major infrastructure project and is considering using steel produced in Ghana. There may be a level of uncertainty about the risk involved in procuring products from that particular geography, so the forecasting tools that Delta Economics provides enable its clients to work out what their risk margin is by producing an assessment of the environment in a quantitative manner. The tools are based on information gathered over many years showing long-term trends. In effect, the data is reducing uncertainty by providing rational evidence to enable more informed decision-making.

▶ The origins of risk management

On a wider scale, risk management is big business, providing work for a variety of experts who advise companies, governments, institutions and organizations on how to define, assess and manage risk. While risk management might seem like a recent phenomenon, the methodologies used to identify and manage risks today are based on early mathematical principles dating back as far as the seventeenth century. Early studies in sixteenth-century Europe led the French mathematicians Pascal and Fermat to develop a theory of probability in the seventeenth century.

Then, according to financial historian Peter Bernstein, Daniel Bernoulli, a Swiss mathematician working with probabilities in the eighteenth century, was the first person to recognize that the calculation of probabilities for games of chance did not adequately reflect the choices people make in everyday life. Bernoulli's reasoning showed that the decisions people made were often based on value judgements as well as logical thinking. This could explain why a person's behaviour could sometimes appear odd to others, depending on the nature of the risk they were taking.

Today, risk experts still grapple with trying to find a way to integrate this 'human behaviour factor' with the scientific and technical or mathematical data when making their risk assessments – and that's what makes the task more challenging.

◗ Decision-making and values

When it comes to making decisions, you may have noted from the Forbes list of hazardous sports in the USA that potential outcomes (injuries from sport) need to be specified clearly enough for an organization or individual to make informed decisions about possible courses of action.

Two things that contribute to how decisions about risk are made are:

▌ the *values* that underpin a judgement

▌ how people *behave in relation to those values* when they make a decision about a course of action.

The following table shows the mortality statistics for England and Wales in 2009. It is likely that this data could be of interest to risk-management specialists working in the area of preventative healthcare. Their input, based on these statistics, could influence a change in government policy and, as a result, the behaviour of the public.

▼ Excerpt from *Mortality Statistics: Deaths Registered in England and Wales*, ONS 2009

Cause of death	Male	Female	2009 total	2008 total
All causes, all ages	238,062	253,286	489,097	506,791
Circulatory diseases	77,636	82,143	159,779	168,238
Cancers and neoplasms	74,016	66,481	140,497	141,143
Respiratory diseases	31,786	35,773	67,559	71,151
Digestive diseases	11,974	13,256	25,230	25,997
Pregnancy and childbirth	0	63	63	44

Compared with 2008, these statistics show a 43 per cent increase in deaths from pregnancy and childbirth and a 5 per cent reduction in deaths from circulatory diseases. If the underlying value is that all deaths are equal, the focus could turn towards reducing mortality rates in pregnancy and childbirth. However, significantly fewer people in England and Wales are affected by this category than, say, by circulatory diseases, so if preventative action were taken to reduce maternal mortality, it might only benefit a small proportion of the population. The question therefore is whether or not that would be the most appropriate course of action.

However, if the underlying value was reducing mortality rates of the young, then policymakers and risk-management specialists might interpret the data differently. This question is part of the long-standing argument about whether to count 'lives saved' or 'life-years saved' when evaluating policies to reduce mortality risk.

When dramatic statistics such as these mortality figures or the numbers of injuries for a sport catch the attention of the media, the resulting publicity drives public concern about a particular issue and this concern often influences government behaviour and policy. When there is a health scare such as BSE or avian flu, the amount of media coverage can be massive and have a dramatic impact on the average person's perception of the level of risk they face. This issue of the communication of risk is considered in more detail in Chapter 6.

▶ The value of a statistical life

Understanding the value of life is a measure that has been historically used by government policymakers as a reference point for measuring the benefits of risk reduction, where citizens' lives are at risk or where the goal is to save lives. Examples range from measuring the potential benefit of draining the swamps near ancient Rome to reduce malaria, to imposing limits on air pollution in developed countries in more recent times.

For example, when major road construction projects have to operate within a budget, those involved have to make decisions about risk versus other factors, such as the number of lanes, congestion times and environmental issues. They use the Value of a Statistical Life (VSL) as a measure for the amount that a group of people is willing to pay for fatal risk reduction, in the expectation of saving one life. In effect, this is about deciding what society is willing to pay for the potential benefits of saving life. But the mere act of placing a financial value on human life can stir up ethical, religious and philosophical questions and it brings us back to the importance of understanding the values behind any definition of risk.

▶ A framework for risk management

When considering how to assess and manage risk, it is worth being aware of how all these elements fit together. The following diagram shows the risk-management process and the typical steps that people take, whether in work or in life.

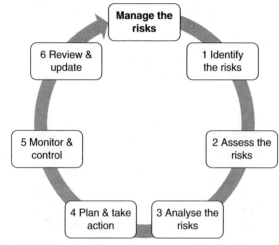

▲ The risk-management process

Consider a simple example of how you would manage the potential risk of getting wet on the way to work if it rains. First of all, you would have to identify whether this is a risk that might occur. It is likely that you would use a variety of data to assess the risk. Depending on what part of the world you live in, there might be a higher or lower chance of rain, so you might know from experience what is likely to happen. You might also use the quantitative data on weather patterns that are available via the Internet or on the TV news. Perhaps your neighbour will comment on the risk as you leave for work, saying, 'It looks like it will rain today', which is a form of qualitative data.

Next, if you analyse the risk based on probability and impact, you might think that, while there is only a 30 per cent chance of rain, it is very important today that you look professional and tidy because you are delivering a pitch to a potential client. So the probability is low, but the impact of getting wet is high. This analysis causes you to pack your umbrella in your briefcase to ensure that you have a solution to mitigate the risk. The following day, you might review and update your action if it looks as if it is going to be sunny and the weather report on TV concurs.

The difference between this type of risk and the type that we perceive as much riskier concerns the impact or consequences of our actions. With weather, for example, you get immediate feedback, but if you are a bond trader and you make some risky decisions today, the consequence of your actions may only become noticeable to others after a much longer period.

Risk and consequences

The story of Nick Leeson is a good example of how taking risks can have a massive impact. In 1993, a year after he began working as a trader for Barings Bank in Singapore, he generated more than £10 million for the company, which was around 10 per cent of the entire profit for Barings that year. But in 1994 his luck ran out and he began to accrue losses, which nine months later had amounted to over £208 million. He hid these losses in a series of obscure accounts and it was not until February 1995, two days before his 28th birthday, that he fled to Malaysia and left a note on his desk that said, 'I'm sorry.' He had accumulated so much financial liability for the bank that Barings immediately collapsed and was sold to Dutch bank ING for £1.

▶ Short term versus long term

Another factor that influences what risks people take is the issue of short-term thinking versus long-term thinking. Using fossil fuels, overeating and cutting corners on safety may all have an appealing short-term outcome, but they can be harmful in the longer term. Thinking only in the short term is a worrying trend that seems to be impinging on many aspects of society.

According to Caspar Berry, international speaker on the subject of risk and a former professional poker player, it's the single biggest reason why people are becoming more risk-averse:

> *Many people are unable to escape the constraints of short-term thinking, and the net effect is they never get used to accepting that failure is part of the process of risk-taking. As a poker player I used to expect that I would lose at least 50 per cent of the hands I played, but that overall there would be enough that I would win to make it a risk worth taking.'*

This issue will be discussed in more detail in Chapter 4.

▶ Perspectives on risk

It is also important to bear in mind whose perspective on risk you are considering when taking an action. What may appear beneficial to one party could be detrimental to another. For example, in 2012 Facebook carried out a secret 'emotional contagion' experiment on 689,003 users, where they are alleged to have edited feeds to highlight either positive or negative posts, which were seen by friends on their newsfeeds. The users' responses were then monitored to see whether these posts had an impact on their friends' attitudes.

This manipulation of data in the name of research demonstrates that it depends on your own perspective on an issue as to how it influences your perception of risk. The Facebook case became front-page news, and the media began asking questions about whether the study contravened any data protection laws; whether it was part-funded by the US government; and the ethics of using the subjects' data without their informed consent; and so on. From the researchers' perspective, they presumably considered it worthwhile to conduct the experiment, with the potential gains outweighing the downsides.

In the earlier Forbes table, cycling was listed as the second most hazardous sport – but was that from the perspective of the cyclist, the motorist or the pedestrian? For example, for drivers and pedestrians, cyclists can certainly be a hazard when they cycle the wrong way along a one-way street, or cycle through a red traffic light. It all depends on perspective.

Summary

This chapter has introduced the various aspects of risk, which the subsequent chapters will explore in more detail.

Understanding our propensity for risk-taking

'Only those who will risk going too far can possibly find out how far one can go.'

T. S. Eliot

In this chapter we explore the human element of risk-taking, and how our personality shapes how we respond to risky situations.

Risk is an integral part of our lives and these days most jobs have an element of risk, as do a number of common daily or regular activities, such as travel. How people respond to risk varies greatly, and how they are typically likely to react to any given risk depends on their risk propensity – their natural temperament – as well as on their risk perception, which is based on their personal experiences.

However, regardless of our typical reactions, familiarity in any situation can lead to comfort and complacency. This can then cause slips or mistakes to occur due to lapses in concentration or fatigue. This is why pilots and surgeons, and others in critical roles where safety is paramount, use checklists. In a study in the US (Pronovost, 2006), a checklist of evidence-based infection-control activities was implemented to reduce the risk of line infections in intensive care unit (ICU) patients. This initiative achieved a remarkable reduction in infections, with many ICUs completely eliminating line infections for months at a time. It showed that, by standardizing a list of steps to be followed, and creating the expectation that every step will be followed for every patient, checklists have the potential to greatly reduce the risk of errors. In effect, they recognized that there can be human error and that we don't always behave consistently 100 per cent of the time, so a checklist can help us to remember critical parts of routine processes.

▲ Using checklists reduces the risk of error

A checklist also helps to avoid potential problems in hierarchical environments where sometimes a subordinate may find it difficult to challenge someone in a position of authority. For example, if a nurse spots a surgeon making an error or forgetting to complete part of a process, the checklist allows for this conversation to take place without 'perceived authority or status' getting in the way.

▶ Prospect theory

The question of inconsistent behaviour is also relevant when we consider how individuals take risks. Research carried out on prospect theory by Daniel Kahneman and Amos Tversky (1979) proposed that risk-taking is inconsistent because people make decisions based on potential losses or gains rather than the final outcome. One of the ways to change an individual's behaviour could be as simple as the way that data is presented – for example, whether a choice of outcome is presented as a loss or a gain. Kahneman describes the following example in his book *Thinking, Fast and Slow* (2011):

▶ Problem 1 – Which do you choose? Get $900 for sure *or* get a 90 per cent chance to get $1,000.

▶ Problem 2 – Which do you choose? Lose $900 for sure *or* get a 90 per cent chance to lose $1,000.

Most people are risk-averse in Problem 1; that is, they would rather get $900 for sure. However, in Problem 2, most people choose to gamble and go for the 90 per cent chance of losing $1,000. Kahneman explains that this is because when all the options appear bad (that is, you will lose money), people are more risk-seeking.

He then goes on to explain that the important additional aspect of prospect theory, compared to earlier research by Swiss mathematician Daniel Bernoulli, is a reference point. This is the state you were in relative to the gains or losses being evaluated. That is, how much money did you have to start off with, before being offered the chance to gain or lose $900? If you stand to lose $900 and you only have $1,000, then it is potentially a greater proportional loss than someone who has $20,000 already and may gain or lose $900. In addition, it is feasible that our propensity for risk-taking varies depending on our experience of taking the risk previously, our emotional state at the time, and new information that may cause us to reconsider our actions. This is perhaps where the saying 'Once bitten, twice shy' is a useful axiom.

▶ Positive risk-taking

A potential disadvantage of the Information Age is that it can induce a false sense of comfort or a heightened sense of fear. The consequence of reacting to information without due consideration and validation is that individuals develop a false perception of risk. Not all risk is bad, and our willingness to take a risk depends how the risk is presented, as highlighted above.

While risk-taking is not a wholly learned skill, because it is partly based on our natural temperament, the ability to gain practice in assessing and taking risks is important in order to develop better judgement over time, and to be more comfortable taking risks with more or fewer potential consequences.

According to world-famous Australian racing driver David Brabham, Triple Le Mans 24-hour class winner and winner of three International Sports Car series,

> 'Your perception of risk changes as you develop experience. It's about the trial and error process you probably experienced as a kid, and when you go over the limit you learn where the boundaries are. I see this in my own son as he is developing as a racing driver. While I might want him to shortcut the route to achieving the success he wants, I know that it will only come through him gaining experience over time, and learning about his capability to take risks.'

One example of where the concept of positive risk-taking can be observed is when a person accepts an opportunity that they believe can lead to progress or a broadening of their experience. In this situation, the often-natural restrictive senses are overcome, which in turn can help to stimulate greater creativity, innovation and confidence. By practising positive risk-taking, you improve your ability to judge good or bad decisions. For example, Chris Blake, in his book *The Art of Decisions* (2008), explains that good poker players do two things better than most other people in terms of positive risk-taking:

1 They lose less money on weak hands, because they are not tempted to fritter away small stakes on poor hands with only a small chance of success.

2 They make more money when they have good hands, because they will risk more to have a chance of winning more when they have a strong hand.

▲ Good poker players practise positive risk-taking

Most poker players use associative reasoning (historical patterns that the unconscious mind notices) along with logical, rule-based assessment that they have built up over thousands of hands to be able to make quick decisions. In other words, they practise, and as a result they get a better feeling for the likely outcomes of different situations.

While the enticement of future rewards may be the motivator for some in terms of risk-taking, it is also widely known that the presence of stress or a highly distressing situation influences the types of decision that individuals make. For example, there is a growing body of evidence from Lerner and Keltner (2000) to suggest that risk-taking behaviour is also influenced by negative states such as fear, anger and dissatisfaction.

▶ Social anxiety and risk-taking

One of these states is described as social anxiety, a subject receiving more attention these days. Social anxiety is discomfort in or fear of social interactions and it involves a concern about being judged or evaluated by others, for example when meeting people in a social situation or meeting people in authority. The latest thinking suggests that, in low emotional states, people display social anxiety through risk-avoidance contexts, but when they are in high emotional states people show social anxiety through risk-seeking. Some researchers conclude that this could be as a way of avoiding the stress associated with the anxiety.

Two examples of this risk-seeking behaviour are drinking alcohol and taking drugs. An article in the *Journal of Anxiety Disorders* (2013) describes two aspects of cognitive resource theory that reflect this thinking on social anxiety and risk-taking:

▶ Under conditions of stress, cognitive resources that regulate our emotions are diverted away from the processes necessary to inhibit risky behaviour, resulting in more risk-taking.

▶ Engagement in risky behaviour serves as a form of negative reinforcement so that the behaviour itself reduces the distress associated with social anxiety.

▶ Risk aversion

In recent times, risk aversion has become a more widely discussed behavioural characteristic, especially in the business and commercial arenas. Risk aversion is the reluctance of a person to accept an outcome with an uncertain pay-off rather than an outcome with a more certain, but possibly lower, expected pay-off. Prospect theory (see above) seeks to explain behaviour that could be described as risk-averse.

Following the economic downturn in developed countries in late 2008, many people have become more risk-averse with their money. A risk-averse investor will put their money in a bank account with a low but guaranteed interest rate instead of investing in the stock market with potentially higher returns but also a higher risk of losing money.

▶ How the media influence behaviour

Dan Gardner, in his book *Risk: The Science and Politics of Fear* (2008), explains how the media shape our judgements and promote fear. He points out that commentary on risk from scientists and the media is received differently: scientists rely on evidence and they are ethically bound to tell the whole truth, and as a result they find that it can be difficult to have their message heard by the wider public; whereas the media know that humans are good with stories and bad with numbers.

We remember the dramatic because it connects with our emotions. When the *Daily Mail* in the UK published an article with the headline 'Smoking just one cannabis joint raises danger of mental illness by 40 per cent', the aim was to provoke an emotional reaction based on fear. The *Daily Mail* article was based on research published in *The Lancet* on cannabis and mental illness, and it was only elsewhere in the small print of the story that it stated that the research did not show that cannabis use *causes* mental illness, but that the two are statistically associated. This means that mental illness could be caused by something else entirely. The headline figure of 40 per cent was also only a **relative risk** – that is, the difference in risk is compared to another group. The more relevant data is the **absolute risk**, which is the probability of that disease occurring over a period of time.

The website www.patient.co.uk describes the difference between relative and absolute risk as follows:

> *'Say men have a 2 in 20 risk of developing a certain disease by the time they reach the age of 60. Then, say research shows that a new treatment reduces the relative risk of getting this disease by 50%. The 50% is the relative risk reduction, and is referring to the effect on the 2. Then 50% of 2 is 1. So this means that the absolute risk is reduced from 2 in 20 to 1 in 20.'*

Once you start to question the way that stories are told in the media, you notice that they generally promote fear, which taps into our emotions and is thus more memorable than purely rational data.

The following list shows the things that American teenagers fear most. Consider to what degree the teenagers may have been influenced by the media rather than their personal experience, bearing in mind that the poll was done in 2005 – four years after 9/11. It is also possible that they made their choices from a predetermined list rather than from their original thinking, which can also make a difference.

▼ 2005 Gallup poll: the top ten things feared most by US teenagers

1. Terrorist attacks	6. Heights
2. Spiders	7. Crime and violence
3. Death	8. Being alone
4. Failure	9. The future
5. War	10. Nuclear war

▶ Risk perception

The way that the public perceives risk is an important, if not vital, subject for a rapidly growing number of people. It used to be just the politicians and policymakers who were concerned with risk perception because it related to such issues as transport and safety. Now it is the psychological analysis of these and other issues – such as public opinion, media coverage, social media, health and the environment – that attracts more interest.

Broadly, researchers have proposed two distinct approaches to explaining risk perceptions:

1 **The psychometric paradigm**, predominantly developed by psychologists

2 **Cultural theory**, proposed by sociologists and anthropologists.

Until recently, these two approaches existed in parallel worlds as the two disciplines worked in isolation from each other, even though it is likely that people are generally able to observe how the different approaches coexist in day-to-day life. It was not until the late 1970s that a number of research groups began to integrate these two approaches and explore broader influences.

Overall, the psychometric paradigm has been a much stronger influence in the psychological research into risk perception than cultural theory, as it has been better at explaining and even at times predicting perceived risk. But, as the demand for trying to mitigate risk continues, so both theories of psychometric paradigm and cultural theory continue to receive considerable attention.

> *'We are living in a world that is beyond controllability.'*
>
> Ulrich Beck

The psychometric paradigm

This approach to risk perception explains how non-experts are likely to view a possible hazard or risk. It suggests that they use a qualitative approach (described in Chapter 1) based on emotion and perception to make intuitive risk assessments. Policy experts, engineers and other specialists often use this approach to get a better understanding of the view of a non-expert, because laypeople can often dismiss or put little credence in risk assessments and data provided by technical experts and government officials. However, this approach can be criticized for the way it aggregates data, which may result in some differences in individual risk perception being missed.

Cultural theory

The cultural theory of risk seeks to predict and explain 'what kind of people will perceive which types of hazards, to be how dangerous' (Wildavsky, 1990). Since the 1980s three major perspectives on this cultural theory have emerged:

1 **Risk society** – this view, based on work by Ulrich Beck, Anthony Giddens and others, proposes that societies are moving into an age where, as a result of industrialization, urbanization and globalization, dangers and hazards have increased significantly. This means that our lives are being dominated by concerns and debates about risk.

2 **Governmentality** – this view is inspired by Michel Foucault's suggestion that modern societies are controlled and organized so that they encourage voluntary participation. Foucault's phrase 'the conduct of conduct' (*'conduire la conduite'*) is the essence of governmentality. His work was advanced by Robert Castel, Ian Culpitt, Mitchell Dean, François Ewald and Pat O'Malley, paying particular attention to the interrelationship between power and subjectivity as well as the language of risk used by societal entities such as governments, policymakers and administrators.

3 **Cultural/symbolic** – the founding proponent of this approach was Mary Douglas, whose Cultural Cognition Project envisaged risks as being part of the shared cultural understandings and practices founded on social expectations and responsibilities.

The Cultural Cognition Project developed a hypothesis, 'The cultural cognition of risk', commonly known as cultural recognition. The project team used scales to measure and assess attitudes that reflected Douglas's preferences about how society should be organized around two dimensions:

▶ **Group** refers to the degree to which individuals are members of particular social units and how absorbing the group's activities are on the individual.

▶ **Grid** refers to the degree of solidarity among members of a society and how much it is regulated and restricted.

When these two options (low to high) are placed on a two-axis system, four different dimensions are created. Depending on the dimension, it will guide that individual's interaction with the environment.

▶ **Individualists** make choices that are unconstrained by society. They value individual initiative, lack close ties to others and fear threats (for example social conflict) that might interfere with free exchange.

▶ **Egalitarians** believe that everyone is equal and that the good of the group comes first. They live in voluntary associations and tend to be sensitive to low-probability–high-consequence risks (such as pollution or new technology) and so can be viewed as 'doommongers'.

▶ **Hierarchists** take the view that there should be well-defined roles and rules plus clear consequences for deviations, because to exceed the limits risks the system collapsing. They accept risk as long as government or experts justify it.

▶ **Fatalists** suffer from a sense of insecurity and so surprises or random events can bring about feelings of being out of control. This, combined with their passive approach, can make them feel – and be – isolated (by others).

In effect, cultural theory shifts the focus away from concepts such as safety and risk and more towards social institutions. This means that, when you are looking at how to deal with risk in a reasonable manner, you must first understand the underlying system and the thinking that guides behaviour.

	Group	
	Weak bonds between people	Strong bonds between people
Many and varied interpersonal differences	**Fatalist**	**Hierarchist**
Significant similarity between people	**Individualist**	**Egalitarian**

▲ The grid–group cultural model

Dan Kahan, Professor of Psychology at Yale Law School and part of the Cultural Cognition Project, further developed Douglas's work and found a high degree of correlation between risk perception and world view. If a person were, say, a hierarchist, you could quite accurately predict how they might approach certain risks.

For example, Kahan found that a disproportionate number of white men were hierarchist or individualist. However, it was not race or gender that mattered, but culture: he reinforced this view when he discovered also that, although black men generally rated the risks of private gun ownership to be very high, those who were individualist rated guns a low risk, just the same as white men who were individualist. Hierarchists and individualists shared similar views on this issue, whereas fatalists and egalitarians felt that private gun ownership was dangerous.

Kahan observed that it was about the cultures and the feelings that those cultures create. When he took his research across cultures, Kahan spotted, for example, that the American egalitarian is much more worried about nuclear power than the French egalitarian. This is because it goes back to the culture and history of a country and how that influences people's perceptions of risk.

▶ System 1 and System 2 thinking

Another factor to pay attention to in understanding how humans make judgements and decisions is to appreciate what may be going on inside the brain when they display irrational behaviour.

The work of Daniel Kahneman, who was awarded a Nobel Prize in economics in 2002, is helpful in this regard. System 1 and System 2 thinking, sometimes colloquially known as 'the law of least effort' (!), has been made popular in part by Kahneman's work, which is described in his best-selling book *Thinking, Fast and Slow* (2011), in which he writes:

> *'We have a very narrow view of what is going on. We don't see very far in the future, we are very focused on one idea at a time, one problem at a time, and all these are incompatible with rationality as economic theory assumes it.'*

An example Kahneman uses to describe irrational behaviour was a study at the National Academy of Sciences, which found that Israeli parole judges, known for turning down parole applications, were more likely to award parole in cases they heard immediately after taking a meal break, when about 65 per cent of requests are granted. Kahneman commented,

> *'Presumably they are hungry, but certainly they are tired, and depleted. When you are depleted, you tend to fall back on default actions, and the default action in that case is apparently to deny parole. So yes, people are strongly influenced by the level of glucose in the brain.'*

Kahneman attributes the irrational behaviour of the parole judges to the different systems that the brain is using to make decisions at the time, which he calls System 1 and System 2 thinking:

▶ **System 1:** Fast, automatic, frequent, emotional, stereotypic and subconscious

▶ **System 2:** Slow, effortful, infrequent, logical, calculating and conscious

When you are actively involved in a task that requires self-control or difficult cognitive reasoning (having to think through a complicated problem or decision), your blood glucose level drops and you are less likely to use System 2. What is effectively happening is that the brain is relying on System 1 to make its decisions. System 1 is fast, intuitive, associative, metaphorical, automatic, impressionistic, and it cannot be switched off. Broadly, System 1 is in part what we 'feel' and so in part it has little sense of intentional control. That said, it is often our primary decision-maker.

Think about how people make a major decision when they are buying a property. Many make their decision based on 'gut feeling' – when they see the front door or the kitchen for the first time (System 1 thinking) and after that it is about justifying the decision. On the other hand, System 2 is slower and more deliberate and it requires effort and reasoning (thinking). (Watch a video entitled 'The Invisible Gorilla' for a great and fun example of how we use System 1 thinking.) When System 2 thinking is used, decisions can take longer and can seem more uncertain and more complex, especially if the options considered are left open and attract undue uncertainty.

▶ Assessing risk-taking and personality

System 1 and System 2 thinking provides insight into the thinking processes of the brain in response to different situations. It is also beneficial to be aware of how personality influences our response to risk-taking because, while we may think we have evolved as humans, in many respects our genetic make-up has largely remained unchanged over the last few thousand years and it is still these roots of personality that influence our behaviour.

After the economic crisis of 2007, which followed the collapse of Barings Bank in 2001 and Lehman Brothers in 2007, those in the financial sector began to pay closer attention to the compliance and regulatory issues that needed to be tightened up. They were also concerned to find better ways to assess the human capital risk. In other words, was it possible to characterize individuals in terms of their propensity for risk-taking? This seemed to be the variable factor that needed to be better understood.

This concern led to the development of the Risk Type Compass™, a personality-based psychometric tool that enabled organizations to identify individuals' approach to risk. Geoff Trickey of the Psychological Consultancy (PCL) validated research into risk that led to the identification of eight distinct risk types. These types are used to define an individual's differences in risk-taking and ability to manage risk.

These eight types are drawn from four of the so-called Big Five dimensions of personality: extraversion, conscientiousness, neuroticism and openness to experience. The fifth dimension – agreeableness – was not included in the Risk Type Compass as there was not enough consistent research data available.

▼ The eight risk types

Risk type	Characteristics
Wary	Very low risk tolerance. Anxious, self-disciplined and cautious, they try to eliminate risk and uncertainty. Fearful that things are bound to go wrong, they seek to control everything.
Prudent	Low risk tolerance. Self-controlled and detailed in their planning, this type is organized and systematic. Conforming and conventional, they are most comfortable with continuity and familiarity.
Deliberate	Average risk tolerance. Systematic and compliant, they tend to be calm, optimistic and self-confident. They experience little anxiety but never walk into anything unprepared.
Composed	High risk tolerance. The composed type is cool-headed and optimistic. Seemingly almost oblivious to risk, they take everything in their stride and bounce back from disaster.
Adventurous	Very high risk tolerance. The adventurous type is both impulsive and fearless. They combine a deeply constitutional calmness with impulsivity and a willingness to challenge convention.
Carefree	High risk tolerance. Spontaneous and unconventional, they are daring, excitement seeking and sometimes reckless. Their impatience and imprudence make life exciting.
Spontaneous	Average risk tolerance. Uninhibited and excitable, they enjoy spontaneity but are distraught when things go wrong. Passion and imprudence make them exciting but unpredictable.
Intense	Low risk tolerance. Highly strung, pessimistic and self-critical, they take things personally and feel defeated when things go wrong.

(Geoff Trickey, PCL Ltd)

There are two major influences on an individual's propensity for risk-taking. Both are deeply rooted in personality and form the basis for the two axes of the Risk Type Compass. The two axes are:

▶ a fear of danger or threat to physical or emotional security

▶ a need for structure, clarity, predictability and concern about ambiguity.

The eight risk types mean that a person may be at either end of one scale (referred to as the four 'pure' risk types: prudent, composed, carefree and intense) or towards one or other extreme on both (the four 'complex' risk types'). The four risk types of wary, deliberate, adventurous and spontaneous are described as 'complex' because they can combine aspects of the neighbouring types. For example, 'wary' will draw characteristics of 'intense' and 'prudent'.

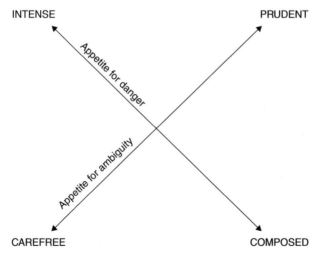

▲ The four pure risk types (Geoff Trickey, PCL Ltd)

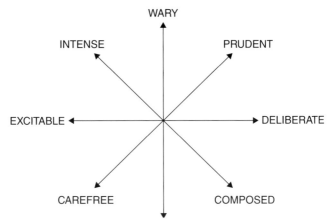

▲ The four complex risk types (Geoff Trickey, PCL Ltd)

Summary

When evaluating our propensity for risk, it is important to consider both our external influences (including political and social groups and the media) and our internal influences (behaviour, preferences and emotional state) to provide a more balanced perspective and suitable response to a risk. The next chapter broadens out from the individual perspective to consider the degree to which we are becoming a risk-averse society.

Are we becoming a risk-averse society?

'Begin challenging your assumptions. Your assumptions are the windows on the world. Scrub them off every once in a while or the light won't come in.'

Alan Alda

The issue of risk pervades modern society in many different ways. From the rules and regulations imposed by governments or organizations in response to potential threats or hazards, to the communication of messages in the media around potential risks and the impact of those messages on the population, we are constantly reminded that we live in an environment full of risks. This chapter will explore the question of to what degree we are becoming a risk-averse society focused on reducing uncertainty.

Broadly, risks can be divided into two types:

▶ **Individual risk** is how individuals view the risk from potential hazards and threats that may affect them personally and that they have some control over – for example travelling in a car.

▶ **Societal risk** is how individuals view the risk from hazards that have an impact on society and over which they have little or no control – for example climate change, pollution and nuclear power.

▶ Information about risk

As we have seen, individuals may vary in their approach to either type of risk as a result of a range of factors. One of these factors is the amount of information they have about the possible consequences versus the likelihood of the risk occurring. You might think that the more information a person has, the easier it is to make a decision, but this is not necessarily true. Other factors may be at work, such as the availability bias, described in Chapter 1. This is when items that are more readily recalled from memory are judged to occur more frequently. For example, if the media have recently been focusing attention on potential terrorist threats to air travel, this is likely to cause some travellers to cancel their plans to fly even though, if they considered it rationally, they might come to a different conclusion. For example, data from the Air Crashes Record Office in Geneva shows a total of 119 aircraft accidents worldwide in 2012 resulting in 794 deaths, which means that it is a far safer form of transport than travelling by car on a motorway.

Information does play an important role in how risks are evaluated, because individuals would rather choose an option with fewer unknown elements than one with many unknown elements. This is known as the Ellsberg Paradox, and it demonstrates what is known as **ambiguity aversion**. If your memory can recall wide media coverage about possible threats regarding air travel, it is likely to have an impact on the action you choose to take.

Another example of how information affects our behaviour can be found in a supermarket. Imagine that we are focused on reducing our input of fat or sugar, to minimize our risk of obesity. When we are presented with a vast array of products with nutritional information, it can be difficult to work out which product contains the least amount of fat or sugar. Even though there are strict regulations for manufacturers to follow about what information needs to be displayed on their product, what can happen in reality is that we become overwhelmed by the information. Then our reaction is to look for a brand we purchased most recently using our System 1 thinking (see Chapter 2) because it is easier for the brain to recall. Alternatively, we make a judgement about the nutritional value of a product based on what we have read, seen or heard in the media. So the availability of information can influence how we view the potential impact of risk to us personally.

If we broaden it out to include societal risk, then the general public often relies on the availability of information to tell them about the potential risks from things over which they have little or no control. They expect the relevant authority or institution to have superior wisdom about the nature of those risks and how to manage them. Scientists in those 'authorities' tend to believe that the public is often inadequately informed about issues such as genetic modification, mobile phones, radioactive waste and food risks, and that they are uninterested in becoming more knowledgeable. In 2001, a study found that 53 per cent of scientists believed that the biggest obstacle to the public gaining more understanding of science was lack of education, while 35 per cent blamed the media and 22 per cent said it was lack of interest. Only a small proportion (20 per cent) of scientists believed that a factor was their own lack of communication skills, and 11 per cent thought that it could be the scientists' lack of interest in communicating with the public. So, regardless of who needs to change (public or scientists), both would agree that the media do play a role in how risk perceptions are created.

▶ Children and young people

As has already been mentioned in this book, when an issue receives a lot of media attention it can lead to the belief that some risks are more pervasive than others. One area where this can be observed in society is in the security of children and young people.

In the UK, the growth of child protection policies has been dramatic. One example of a measure introduced to minimize risk was the Safeguarding Vulnerable Groups Act in 2006. This introduced a new bureaucracy to regulate contact between children or vulnerable groups and adult workers and volunteers. This Act was put into place following an enquiry into the 2002 Soham Murders, which involved two schoolchildren aged 10.

In his book *No Fear* (2007), which focuses on growing up in a risk-averse society, Tim Gill states:

> '... the UK Government estimates that the safeguarding regulations will extend mandatory vetting to over 2 million volunteers and workers involved in sports and leisure, and over 200,000 school governors. The Government has not given any estimates of how many cases of child abuse will be prevented, though it admits that the "the new scheme on its own will not completely prevent all such abuse in the workplace".'

Another area that affects children and young people and which is a source of worry for adults is technology, and in particular the Internet. A Demos report (Green & Hannon, 2007) showed that, for some children and young people, the Internet is not just a medium for entertainment and social networking but also a new territory for creativity, exploration and adventure. In particular, the report described those young people as digital pioneers who are developing new ways of sharing, developing and creating content. Although advances in technology may bring about many possible benefits for children in terms of information gathering and informal learning, their parents are more fearful of the potential online threats from explicit sexual images, online child sexual abuse, cyber-bullying and videos or other content that can upset or traumatize children.

▲ Parents fear the possible risks of Internet use

The advice given by child safety agencies on how to reduce risk was that limited personal information should be disclosed online. However, this potentially flies in the face of today's reality in terms of how children use the Internet in their everyday lives. It is likely that children's computer usage will continue to increase over time, not remain static. This means that, in terms of risk reduction, there is a need for governments and institutions to provide adequate regulation and for parents as well as children and young people to be aware of the possible risks and mitigate them.

▶ Encouraging risk-taking

Despite attempts by society to reduce certain types of risk to children and young people, risk-taking is an important part of their development, and we can still encourage young people to take risks by offering them opportunities to get involved in adventurous activities. One example is the Duke of Edinburgh's Award, a youth charity running programmes in more than 140 countries around the world. Since it was founded in 1956, there have been over 8 million participants globally, and over 2.3 million awards have been achieved. Part of the programme involves an expedition, and it is an effective way for young people to get involved in what might be regarded as an adventurous or 'risky' activity such as kayaking or hiking. As motor racing driver David Brabham says, 'People only really learn about risk through their own experiences, and information does not mean much to them until they have gone out and done it for themselves.'

Another example of learning by experience is the Risk Factory, an initiative funded by four local authorities in Scotland. Their programmes for pupils of 11–12 years old are based on the principle that learning by experience is more memorable than being told what to do. They state that 'pupils are put into scenarios that they could face in everyday life and are taught strategies that could help save not only their own lives but other people's. It allows them to make mistakes but in a safe environment where they can learn from their mistakes.' Their programme consists of 11 scenarios that cover antisocial behaviour, home safety, water safety, electricity, building sites, farms, fire safety, public transport (bus and rail), road safety and Internet safety.

Other ways that children can learn about risk-taking include participation in school trips, as well as learning how to cycle and swim safely. While some of these traditionally organized activities may be on the decline, they do still serve to teach children about how to take risks and push their boundaries. However, they should not be a substitute for the role that parents and family can have in developing a young person's attitude to risk-taking and making decisions around risk.

▌ Risk and society

The observations made so far in this chapter generally concern society at a regional or local level. It is also relevant to consider risk from a more strategic worldwide view, and to see whether there are any differences between developed and developing societies in terms of risk management.

Risk management in Bangladesh

Bangladesh suffers frequent tropical cyclones, and since the 1970s, three large cyclones have hit the country, resulting in between 170,000 and 300,000 deaths from each cyclone. However, once the government and the population became more proactive, there were only 4,000 deaths when a similar typhoon hit in 2007. The country increased the number of its shelters from 12 to 2,500 as well as developing a forecasting system and a method of warning the population. By taking action to mitigate the risks, the country has achieved a big reduction in the number of deaths from cyclones.

According to the World Development Report 2014, entitled 'Risk and Opportunity: Managing Risk for Development', better risk management can be a powerful instrument for the development of a society. The report states that many countries need to change the way they approach risk management: changing behaviour so that it is proactive rather than reactive can save lives and avoid economic setbacks.

Policymakers therefore need to stop being reactive and become more proactive, which involves:

- understanding the risks that a community or country faces – that is, acquiring knowledge

- deciding on what actions to take to protect a country from risks

- considering the option of insurance.

It is also known that, in developing countries, there is often a stronger sense of community, which means that people who decide to take risks are supported by their family, sometimes both financially and emotionally.

Other examples of effective risk reduction have occurred in countries including Peru, Kenya and the Czech Republic. These countries adopted a prudent approach to their finances, which meant they had a disciplined monetary policy and lower fiscal deficits. As a result they were able to cope with the global financial crisis better than their counterparts when it hit in 2008.

▶ Technology's role in reducing risk

Technology can play a useful role in helping both governments and individuals to gain an early warning of potential risks, thus enabling them to take appropriate action. An example in the World Development Report shows that farmers in Ghana and 15 other African countries now receive specific market information through their mobile phones that helps them respond more quickly to changes in demand or prices.

Technology can also bring unexpected benefits to individuals as well as reducing risk to others. It can also reduce the risk of corruption and ensure that employees receive the correct salary. For example, M-Pesa is a mobile-phone-based money transfer and micro-financing service first launched by Vodafone in Kenya. There, the technology has helped reduce the risk of money earned by women either being spent by others or getting into the 'wrong hands'. Previously, when women were paid in cash, their husbands would often take their wives' money to buy alcohol or other personal items. Following the introduction of electronic payment transactions, men no longer had easy access to cash, reducing the risk of the money going 'astray'. The women stated that they also benefited from the change, because they were more likely to save money to build up financial resources for future needs such as sending their children to school.

▲ Mobile phones allow secure money transfers in many countries

In 2008 the M-Pesa service was launched in Afghanistan to pay the salaries of the policemen. The Afghan National Police quickly realized that, under the previous cash payment model, 10 per cent of the employees had been 'ghost' police officers who did not exist, and others had pocketed the salaries. When the new system was introduced, many policemen believed there had been an error as their salaries significantly increased.

▶ Uncertainty avoidance

There appears to be a difference in how developed and developing cultures approach risk. More advanced cultures are becoming more risk-averse, and developing cultures less so. The cultural dimension called 'uncertainty avoidance' seems to be higher in more developed societies than in those that are developing. This concept can be described as the extent to which a society, organization or group relies on social norms, rules and procedures to alleviate the unpredictability of future events, and it has been studied in detail by Geert Hofstede and others.

▼ Societal levels of uncertainty avoidance

High uncertainty avoidance societies	Low uncertainty avoidance societies
▶ use formality in interactions with others	▶ use informality in interactions with others
▶ are orderly and keep meticulous records	▶ are less orderly and keep fewer records
▶ rely on formalized policies and procedures	▶ rely on informal norms for most matters
▶ take moderate, carefully calculated risks	▶ are less calculating when taking risks
▶ show strong resistance to change	▶ show only moderate resistance to change

Hofstede's Uncertainty Avoidance Index gives countries a ranking based on a score between 1 and 120. Countries with a high score tend to maintain rigid codes of belief and behaviour and are intolerant of unorthodox behaviour and ideas. Lower-scoring societies tend to have a more relaxed attitude in which practice counts more than principles.

The highest-scoring countries include Greece (112), Portugal (104), Guatemala (101), Uruguay (100) and Belgium (94), with the lowest-scoring countries being Singapore (8), Jamaica (13), Denmark (23) and Sweden (29).

How does this relate to risk?

Germany has a reasonably high score (65) compared to the USA (46) and the United Kingdom (35). It shows that low-scoring societies are generally higher risk-takers compared to high-scoring societies. For example, the credit crunch began in the USA (a relatively low-scoring country), whereas Belgium (a high-scoring culture) is a country where the level of risk involved in mortgages is almost nil.

Risk in the USA

While the USA may appear to be less calculating when taking risks compared to some other societies, according to the Uncertainty Avoidance Index there seems to have been a change there since the economic downturn. In 2013 a *Wall Street Journal* article by Ben Casselman reported that the US appeared to be turning soft on risk and, as a result, the economy is less dynamic. Fewer people are changing jobs, investors are putting less money into new ventures, and companies are slower to take on new staff. It is these types of activities that enable an economy to adapt to the needs of a changing market.

The article went on to say that the risk-taking spirit still prevails, but it has been focused on specific industry sectors and geographies. Coastal cities and college towns where there is interest in technology or energy seem to be the places that are still a hotbed for entrepreneurial talent willing to take risks, according to Dane Stangler, Director of Research and Policy at the Ewing Marion Kauffman Foundation. The reluctance to take risks is noticeable in the number of US migrations, particularly those between states, according to census data, and that is one of the factors that drives fewer people to change jobs.

According to the *New Statesman* (Robb, 2014), the millennial generation (defined as 21–36-year-olds) is financially more risk-averse than any other age group apart from their grandparents. In January 2014, the UBS investment bank published a study of over 2,500 investors showing that Millennials are among the most financially conservative Americans: 13 per cent of Millennials defined their own risk tolerance as 'conservative', compared to 6 per cent of respondents from Generation X (37–48), 10 per cent of baby boomers (49–67) and 15 per cent of the 68-plus crowd. The reasons for Millennials' economic caution seem to be clear: growing up during a recession is likely to leave most people wary.

Summary

How individuals respond to risk will depend on the world around them and what they observe in terms of risk-taking. Society also plays a role in how people assess and manage risk, with some more developed societies relying more on formal policies and procedures than those that are less developed. In the next chapter, risk in the business world will be addressed, along with the complexities of how it is managed.

4

Risk in the business world

'To win, you have to risk loss.'

Jean-Claude Killy

Success is often quoted as being the result of great preparation and a bit of luck. In the business world, risk has traditionally been considered, or assumed, to be the primary prerogative of large corporations or businesses where the consequence of their service could mean human danger or high financial risk. Airlines, rail companies, banks, food manufacturers and many other different types of business have to follow stringent regulations to ensure that customers and users of their products do not face undue risks.

Over the last few decades the emphasis on risk has increased, and it is not uncommon to have risk assessments conducted across a wide range of activities, from the micro – project planning to small business loans – right through to macro – the environmental impact of global IT companies running massive data centres to store customers' data in 'the cloud'. Consequently, the subject of risk has boomed, resulting in a rapidly growing industry of analysts, specialists, advisers, consultants and new job roles in organizations.

To understand the potential risks facing a business, the business itself must be well understood, and even that will not provide the whole answer because the external environment has an impact too. These external uncertainties may be quantified using sophisticated analysis or through the experience and 'gut feel' of the business leader and their team.

Even events that happen extremely rarely (low probability) are likely to have a major impact on a business (high consequence), but they may not be factored into any risk assessment. For example, terrorism had a huge impact on the financial traders operating near the Twin Towers in New York in 2001.

To take a 'broad brush' view of types of risks in a business, we can use a high level of categorization:

1 Reputational

2 Compliance

3 Operational

4 Financial

5 Strategic

As a business reviews its strategy against these five risk categories, a list of more specific risk activities will become apparent.

▶ Reputational risk

A company's reputation is one of its most important intangible assets:

▶ 70 per cent of consumers avoid buying products if they don't like the company.

▶ 60 per cent of a business's market value is attributable to its reputation.

A study conducted in 2011 by the PR firm Weber Shandwick found that the company behind the brand is critical to consumer purchasing decisions. If they do not like the parent company, 70 per cent of consumers surveyed will avoid buying its products, and 87 per cent of corporate leaders agreed that 'a strong corporate brand is just as important as strong product brands'. Their report went on to suggest six 'new realities of corporate reputation', which are:

1 **Corporate brand is as important as the product brand(s).**

People care about the companies behind the brands they buy. For consumers and executives alike, the reputation of a company is perceived as more important than positive financial earnings.

2 **Corporate reputation provides product quality assurance.**

Products benefit because of strong corporate reputations. Consumers are exerting greater control over what brands they buy, with over two-thirds of consumers avoiding products made by companies they do not like and checking labels to see who the parent company is.

3 **Any disconnect between corporate and product reputation triggers sharp consumer reaction.**

In the study, 54 per cent of consumers reported being surprised to find that a product or service they liked was made by a company they did not like.

4 **Products drive discussion, with reputation close behind.**

The study found that 69 per cent of consumers frequently or regularly discuss how they feel about a product they bought. These discussions cover customer service, how employees are treated, company scandals and their feelings about the company's reputation.

▼ Weber Shandwick report extract, 2012

What topics do consumers frequently or regularly discuss with others?	%
How you feel about a product you have purchased	69
The quality of specific companies' customer service	55
How specific companies treat their employees	45
News about a scandal or wrong-doing at specific companies	43
How you feel about a company as a whole / its reputation	40
News about good deeds a specific company does	37
The financial performance of specific companies	33
How specific companies are using social media	32
What specific companies are doing to protect the environment	31
Specific companies' websites	30
What specific companies are doing to help those in their communities	29
Specific corporate leaders, such as CEOs or other executives	28

5 Consumers shape reputation instantly.

According to 88 per cent of consumers, word of mouth is the leading influence on them forming opinions of companies. Online reviews and online search results are also important.

6 Corporate reputation contributes to company market value.

Most admired status carries more weight than financial earnings. Executives estimate that, on average, 60 per cent of their firms' market value is attributable to its reputation.

With the almost exponential increase in the use of social media, it is very easy for a message to go viral and spread around the world extremely quickly. Negative publicity can seriously affect a company's reputation and brand, and can erode the value of the business very quickly.

Malaysia Airlines

Sometimes the reputation of a company can be tarnished by a factor outside its control. In 2014, two Malaysia Airlines planes were lost in tragic circumstances, causing analysts to speculate that it could make it difficult for the airline to continue operating. Directly following the crash of MH17 en route from Amsterdam to Kuala Lumpur, shares in Malaysia Airlines closed 11 per cent down. Despite receiving the 'best airline in Asia' accolade in 2013 at the World Travel Awards, some analysts commented that the second incident, so soon after the disappearance of MH370, 'will now compromise the brand from a European perspective and you've got to ask whether the brand can survive this latest tragedy'.

The Malaysia Airlines case is an example of how external events can have a major impact on a company's reputation. More often than not, however, it is a factor within the control of a business or individual that negatively impacts its reputation.

There are many examples of sports stars whose behaviour 'off the field' has potentially had a negative impact on the reputation of the sport, and as a result their sponsors have dropped them. Nike withdrew their sponsorship of Lance Armstrong when there was 'seemingly insurmountable evidence' from the US anti-doping agency that Armstrong has used performance-enhancing drugs.

▶ Compliance risk

The following extract from the American Bar Association (2003) offers a useful context to the rise in prominence of compliance risk.

> 'The business world had leaped from the financial section to Page One. The alleged accounting fraud at Enron was so massive that it brought down one of the nation's largest companies. Then the story expanded to include allegations of obstruction of justice at Arthur Andersen.
>
> Suddenly, there seemed to be an endless succession of corporate scandals: Adelphia, Tyco, ImClone, Xerox, Rite-Aid, WorldCom. The trend has been so extensive that it may be undermining the entire capital market. Instead of a single storm sinking a few ships and passing on out to sea, it appears the impact is closer to a corporate Watergate – an event that causes fundamental rethinking of society's assumptions.'

The risk to a company of not conforming to laws, regulations or prescribed practices is that its profits or capital can be threatened and it may be subject to fines, payment of damages and voided contracts, which can result in a negative impact on its reputation. In some situations this can lead to a company being unable to enforce its contracts and, as a result, it can mean devaluation or, worse, closure for the company.

Since the late 1990s the business disciplines of compliance, governance and risk management have increasingly shared similar activities, focusing on areas such as operational risk, internal audits and incident and crisis management. Consequently, many major corporations now integrate these three disciplines into a collective activity: governance, risk management and compliance (GRC).

In the banking industry, compliance risk – or, as it is sometimes known, integrity risk – is closely aligned to reputation; banks' adherence to principles of integrity and fair dealing is therefore of paramount importance in defining their value. The Basel Committee on Banking Supervision [BCBS] is a committee of banking supervisory authorities that was established by the central bank governors of the Group of Ten Countries in 1974. BCBS provides a forum for regular co-operation on banking supervisory matters. Its objective is to enhance understanding of key supervisory issues and improve the quality of banking supervision worldwide. Following the financial crisis in late 2008, the Basel Committee set higher standards for minimum capital requirements that banks need to hold as a protection against losses. This meant that the ratio of equity capital to assets rose from 2 to 7 per cent. However, the Committee has given banks up to 1 January 2018 to comply with the new standard.

▶ Operational risk

Operational risk is often a more prominent descriptor used by organizations. It includes legal risk, but not strategic or reputational risk. Central to operational risk is the risk of loss due to internal processes, people and systems issues or from external sources such as earthquakes, floods, power failures and terrorism. If a company has outsourced arrangements, then careful management is required around the control aspects of the arrangements, and in particular loss of continuity of supply.

Poor operational risk management: a case study

A small business was using 'the cloud' to store sensitive financial data. Their IT provider informed them that there was a problem with the storage, which meant that they were unable to access their data for a number of days. This seriously reduced their ability to trade. As a result, mistrust arose between the supplier and the business, even though the problem might have been caused by an external event outside anyone's control rather than lack of attention or carelessness. The small business had mistakenly assumed that they were reducing their risks by storing the data offsite, and had taken no further steps to mitigate potential risks.

A priority for a management team is to secure their business from operational risks. Loss of intellectual property, let alone life or physical assets, can be devastating to a business's performance and reputation. Business leaders need to identify, evaluate and mitigate the company's operational risk.

Social media allow people to convey their feelings of mistrust about an organization to a wide audience quickly and easily, posing a risk to that organization.

Many customers who experience frustration at the lack of service when communicating with call centres or large companies often take to Twitter or Facebook to share their views with the wider public. This is why many multinationals employ people to monitor and respond to social media comments related to their organization, because they cannot risk any damage to their reputation or a negative impact on their operations.

To reduce operational risk successfully, it is important to develop good practice in managing such risk by:

▶ not allowing business confidence to dull the senses that inform the portfolio of business risks

▶ ensuring that the business is secure at all levels and regularly challenging assumptions

▶ monitoring, managing and practising the consequences of changes in risk levels

▶ understanding the business impact of risks – for example in response levels, recovery rates and reputational resilience.

▶ Financial risk

One of the most common and significant elements of financial risk is credit risk. This is because credit risk underpins a business's stability, growth and future profitability.

There are numerous credit measurement and scoring models that businesses can use. The CAMPARI framework is one of the more popular ones that some banks use to assess loan applications from small businesses or individuals. It also offers a useful framework for business leaders to evaluate the credit health of their company:

C – Character

A – Ability to repay

M – Means and resources to run the business

P – Purpose

A – Amount

R – Repayment

I – Insurance and interest

The CAMPARI framework can be seen in action in the UK television programme *Dragon's Den*. In this show, entrepreneurs with great business ideas pitch for funding to a group of potential investors. As well as understanding the business opportunity that the entrepreneurs are pitching, the investors are interested in the journey the entrepreneurs have been on with their business idea to arrive at the Dragon's Den. They are also evaluating the 'character' of the entrepreneur because the bottom-line question for the investor is, 'Can I trust this person with my investment?'

Another example showing the usefulness of the CAMPARI model is the story of a bank manager who, early in his career, had to decide whether to grant a loan to a bank customer. The applicant was friendly and confident and seemed to have the ability to repay. The bank manager authorized the loan but the customer then disappeared and the loan was never repaid. The bank manager realized he had been taken in by the person's character and had not sufficiently analysed the 'ability to repay' element of the CAMPARI model. The lesson was a valuable learning opportunity for the bank manager, who had failed to consider all the risk factors. This did not deter him from taking risks again because he learned from this experience to use all the elements of the model.

▶ Quantifying risks

Identifying risks that have a financial impact may seem easy to do, but quantifying them is often more difficult. If you also consider broader sociopolitical and geopolitical influences, it becomes even trickier.

'If you look at the world businesses work in, they work in an environment of uncertainty; they don't know what will happen in the next minute.'

Rebecca Harding, CEO, Delta Economics

Several companies provide a general advisory risk service, which can cover both opportunities and risks in the business environment, particularly at a global level. Increasingly, though, assessment and analysis are not enough for businesses; they want quantification of the types of risk they face, in particular the geopolitical risks since these have the most impact on economic and trade growth.

▲ Rebecca Harding, Delta Economics

There are now specialist companies that help other businesses to quantify risks using modelling. One example is Delta Economics, founded by Dr Rebecca Harding, an economist, who says:

> 'We use trade data to quantify risk, because it represents business growth and business aspects that measure what is going on in the real economy. We analyse the market environment, the pricing environment, long-term economic development, the business environment, the political environment and the economic environment as well as measures

of risk from a social media aspect which today also needs close scrutiny. This analysis enables organizations to have a quantifiable number that they can factor into their own risk models and then calculate the insurable risk, which can make their environment more certain.'

Small businesses, by their very nature, are often fairly vulnerable to risk, but they may not give the issue close attention. A small business should take these steps to minimize risk:

▶ **Manage cash flow** – being cash-conscious and not relying on gut feeling, using a comprehensive cash-flow forecast to manage the business

▶ **Insure key personnel** – insuring key people against death or critical illness. In the UK, the chances of dying during working life are 1 in 7 for men and 1 in 11 for women, so, depending on the business's appetite for risk, this insurance is worth serious consideration.

▶ **Insure against specific risks** – (i) checking that there is adequate breadth and depth of cover for risks that can have a significant impact on a business and (ii) when the nature of the business changes, e.g. with international trading, a new market sector or new technology, to re-evaluate insurances

▶ **Ensure contractual indemnity** – ensuring that business contracts provide for (i) the opportunity to exit from arrangements under specific changes in conditions and (ii) claims against damage caused by other businesses and resources that a business regularly relies upon.

▶ **Create a separate legal entity** – considering creating a separate legal entity if a new venture increases financial, legal or relationship (e.g. partnership)

▶ Strategic risk

Strategic risks are those associated with operating in a particular industry. The risks could come from a competitor moving into the sector, potential mergers or acquisitions, changes in the industry due to legislation, or changes in the customer's demands.

The leadership team of an organization needs to be aware of the wider business environment in order to get early warning of potential issues that could pose a strategic risk to them. Of course, these risks can bring opportunity as well as threats. For example, there are believed to be more than £45 million worth of fake £1 coins circulating in the UK. The government decided that, in order to tackle the problem, they would introduce a new bimetallic coin by 2017, as this type of coin is difficult to replicate as a fake. This decision means that it is likely to cost the country up to £20 million to change things like slot machines, parking meters, shopping trolleys and vending machines.

This type of situation will pose strategic risks to organizations such as local councils, which suddenly may have a huge increase in costs to adapt machines such as parking meters. At the same time it can provide opportunity for others, who can potentially stand to profit from the change.

Influence of the media on business risk

Other strategic issues that a business might face can be as a result of the influence of the media in focusing attention on a particular aspect of their business. While companies can pay close attention to the risk areas described earlier, the media also have a strong influence on business and how it is portrayed. This can mean that a company's best intentions to manage risk can be derailed by media stories, which can stir up highly emotional responses in the general public. The Brent Spar story is a good example of this.

Shell, Brent Spar and the media

In 1995, Shell was embroiled in a public dispute over the decommissioning and disposal of the Brent Spar, a redundant oil storage installation in the North Sea. Shell conducted formal consultations with conservation bodies and fishing interests alongside their own internal risk management, to come up with the most appropriate method. The decision was to dispose of Brent Spar using deep-sea disposal, so the company submitted an Abandonment Plan to the UK Government, which was approved.

Through media influence, Greenpeace challenged the decision, asserting that the Abandonment Plan would lead to deep-sea toxic waste disposal. As the media coverage grew and other governments waded in, Shell faced strong public opposition to the plan in continental northern Europe. Consequently, Shell abandoned the plan and, with the help of the Norwegian authorities who allowed Brent Spar to be anchored in the deep waters of Erfjord, they had to come up with a new solution.

During the next phase, which Shell called 'One Way Forward', they reviewed their accountabilities, working with and through the media and a range of public bodies to evolve a better solution for the disposal of Brent Spar. Shell described the Brent Spar project end as 'not just a North Sea installation but a unique and defining event. The challenge now is to ensure that it defines a new stage in the regulation of business activity that enjoys the popular support of hearts as well as minds.'

Perhaps what the company had not given sufficient initial consideration to was the influence of the media and public opinion. In 2008 they stated that Brent Spar was 'damaging to our reputation: despite the support of independent scientists for our proposals, we did not win public acceptance. We recognized that we needed to change our approach – not just to offshore decommissioning in the UK but to how we conduct our operations everywhere.'

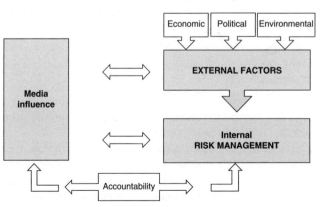

▲ The complex nature of assessing business risk

The model above highlights the complex number of interests to be considered in managing business risk. Traditionally, companies carried out comprehensive risk assessments (internal risk management) and also paid attention to the broader economic, political and environmental factors. What they are now waking up to is the power and influence of the media in issues related to risk, and the importance of engaging stakeholders (whoever they may be) using all means, including social media. Companies now appear to be held accountable to the media as much as to their shareholders, employees and customers.

▶ Risk and the 'war for talent'

Another example of how this model highlights the broader issues of risk is in the recruitment and retention of staff, otherwise known as 'the war for talent'. There is a risk that, if an organization does not attract the brightest and best graduates, it may miss out on the new ideas, innovations and capabilities that talented individuals can bring to a business.

Today's generation expects more from employers, as the senior vice-president of a global multinational recently learned. She wanted to assess the quality of the candidates applying for jobs in the graduate scheme and decided to be part of the interview process. Her previous experience of a job interview was that the company representatives generally had the upper hand and asked challenging questions of the candidates to see whether they made the grade. However, she quickly realized that the young adults of the millennial generation (born between the early 1980s and the early 2000s) have quite different expectations. They asked her to explain why the multinational was a good place to work and why the applicant should consider it as a possibility. Another person asked why the corporation had dropped out of the list of top ten companies to work for and what it was doing in terms of its corporate and social responsibility.

She found the process challenging, not just for the candidates but for her personally too, as well as for the corporation's reputation. It was not just financial reward that enticed the graduates; they were also interested in the broader reputation of the business. Many of their questions and perceptions about the company's brand were based on what they had learned from the Internet, social media and their peers. This is another example of how a business or organization can fail to recognize the potential power and influence of the media – and to take steps to manage this risk appropriately – which can ultimately have a negative impact on bottom-line results.

▶ Other areas of risk

There are three other areas of risk worth mentioning: sustainability risk, environment risk and cyber risk.

Sustainability risk

In Chapter 3, risk was described in two ways – as individual risk and societal risk. While a business might perceive that there is little or no relation between business and society, in fact they are highly interconnected. Increasingly, corporates are required to say something about their sustainability in their annual reports, and some also state how socially responsible they have been. This is relevant to risk because a business is unlikely to be sustainable over the long term if it does not consider the wider environment in which it operates.

In 1994, John Elkington, the founder of a UK consultancy Sustainability, introduced the phrase 'the triple bottom line'. Elkington's view was that businesses should be preparing three distinctly different bottom-line measures:

1 **Profitability**, as defined through the traditional measure of corporate profit from the profit and loss account

2 **People account**, a measure of how socially responsible an organization has been across all its operations

3 **Planet account**, a measure of how environmentally responsible the organization has been.

The aim of a 'triple bottom line' is to provide a framework in which a business, whether run for profit or not, can measure its financial, social and environmental performance over a period of time. Elkington believed that it is only when organizations produce a 'triple bottom line' set of accounts, considering all the costs of conducting their business rather than just the predominant financial performance aspect, that they get a truly holistic picture of their impact.

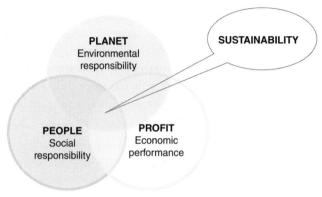

▲ The 'triple bottom line'

Reflecting on this 'triple bottom line' concept in terms of risk and how the world has evolved over the last 20 years, what were the risks that have prevented investors and business leaders from adopting this approach? Measures around people and planet accounts may be difficult to generate, yet some corporations have key performance indicators and job objectives that align with these two bottom-line account approaches.

What is known is that, with clear and purposeful intention, progress could have been made, reported and recognized. However, the overall performance and risk drivers for organizations were not – and to a large extent are still not – aligned for this to occur. Perhaps business is too focused on short-term thinking and therefore ignoring the potential implications for the future until it is too late. Is this a real problem or risk for the planet?

Ultimately, it is risk factors that affect our evolution, but the challenge is always between short-term pleasure and indeterminate long-term risk. Immediate pleasure will always win, says Professor Hugh Montgomery: 'People think that if I drink this, if I smoke this, I cannot quantify the potential risk on my future health and well-being, so I will continue behaving as I am now.'

In business, it is perhaps the same. In the short term, despite awareness of well-reasoned arguments to support a broader bottom-line approach, there is a stronger pull to maintain existing behaviour. The issue of how to influence large-scale behaviour change is discussed further in Chapter 6.

Environment risk

Environment risk is also something for businesses to consider, particularly as part of the planet account. As valuable natural resources decline, their scarcity will have an impact on companies that rely on these resources. In the World Economic Forum list of the top ten risks of highest concern in 2014, these issues were included:

▶ #3 Water crises

▶ #5 Failure of climate change mitigation and adaptation

▶ #6 Greater risk of extreme weather events.

See Chapter 6 for the full list.

▲ Failure to mitigate climate change brings risks to the environment

Organizations are becoming increasingly aware of how climate change could affect their profitability, and many are beginning to future-proof their business against climate change by creating a sustainable roadmap for balancing supply and demand.

Water scarcity affects over 2.7 billion people for at least a month every year. In response to this fact, Professor Arjen Hoekstra has developed the 'water footprint'. It is an indicator of the volume of fresh water used to produce a product, taking into account the volumes of water consumed and polluted in the different steps of the supply chain. Using this approach, it takes 1,000 litres of water to produce 1 litre of milk, and 2,500 litres of water to product 1 kilo of rice. For supermarkets and food suppliers, both rainfall and fresh water are major factors in fresh food supply, so considering our water footprint per country is not only a vital statistic but it also represents a vital resource.

Hoekstra believes that it will be difficult to see quick progress if governments do not force companies to manage and improve their water footprint. He says:

> *'Despite good efforts undertaken by several companies, it is unlikely that the business sector as a whole will sufficiently regulate itself. There is an urgent need for governmental regulation and international co-operation.'*

As the latest IPCC report highlights, adaptation strategies can help alleviate the impacts of climate change. However, because of past emissions, these strategies are not enough. Other action needs to be taken if emission levels are to be reduced. As the World Resources Institute said in 2008, 'Global warming may dominate headlines today. Ecosystem degradation will do so tomorrow.' This remains as true today as it was then and the WRI's 2012 report continues to stress the relevance of ecosystem degradation to business, in terms of its effect on business opportunities and the services business depends on, directly or indirectly.

Cyber risk

As business becomes more reliant on the Internet and cloud-based computing, there is a growing awareness of the importance of IT security. Many employees bring their own smartphones and tablet computers to their place of work, and are sometimes even using them for business-related activities. All this serves to increase the need to manage the risk in terms of cyber security and data protection.

According to Dell:

▶ a laptop is stolen every 53 seconds

▶ 46 per cent of stolen laptops contain confidential data

▶ 90 per cent of them are not protected or have no encryption features.

It is not just business that has to protect itself in cyberspace. Governments also are using the Internet to deliver more of their services to citizens, and therefore there is an expectation that these will not be tampered with or compromised by criminals and hackers. For example, in the UK, Universal Credit will provide support to around 19 million citizens across 8.5 million households, and will include provision of online access to benefit-related services and information. Individuals therefore expect government to take adequate precautions to protect the data and ongoing provision of the service.

Chapter 6 covers the issue of cyber security further, in relation to the global risks of the future.

> '*Music is the silence between the notes.*'
>
> *Claude Debussy*

The business world can be viewed as being surrounded by risk and uncertainty. Equally, it can be viewed as being rich with opportunity and excitement. Could a business be better prepared to deal with risks if it adapted

Debussy's quote above, and learned to play the spaces between the music as loudly as they play the music?

Summary

As reported by Reuters, on 26 September 2001 Enron Chairman Kenneth Lay had an online chat with his employees, during which he said:

'The company is fundamentally sound. The balance sheet is strong. Our financial liquidity has never been stronger... My personal belief is that Enron stock is an incredible bargain at current prices and we will look back a couple of years from now and see the great opportunity that we currently have.'

Less than three months later the company filed for bankruptcy. The various risks discussed in this chapter had not been adequately heeded.

Risk management

'Insanity is losing your glasses in the street but looking for them in your lounge because it's better lit and it's warmer.'

Steven Heller and Terry Steele,
Monsters and Magical Sticks *(2001)*

No matter where we are – at home, at work or elsewhere – risk is something we come across all the time. Dealing with risk is an everyday part of life and not something special that only a few people encounter.

There are some common human tendencies in relation to risk behaviour, which are useful to keep in mind when reading this chapter:

▶ We assess risk based on emotion as well as logic.

▶ Peer pressure can be stronger than a feeling of 'doing good for society'.

▶ Immediate pleasure tends to outweigh indeterminate risk in the long term.

Sometimes we are aware of the risks we take and on other occasions we are not. The risk recognition, assessment and decision-making process happens quickly and it may not register in our minds as such – instead, it's a 'normal/acceptable' reaction to a situation. This chapter will explore how different people use different approaches to risk management, and what some of the issues are for organizations in order for them to be aware of the wide-ranging nature of risks.

▶ Risk management in business

Risk management is of particular relevance in business. It can be defined as 'the identification, analysis, assessment, control, and avoidance, minimization, or elimination of unacceptable risk'.

For those with responsibility for risk management within an organization, their specialism lies in the detailed knowledge of certain types of risk and the ability to consider the options surrounding the probability and possible consequences of the risk. It is important to the success of every organization. Whether it is adapting to change or taking a risk, very few businesses will thrive without doing one or both of these things on a regular basis. Evolution does not stand still; nor does success. Threats and vulnerabilities are key drivers of risk, so continual vigilance and understanding of the world around us is essential. This means that appropriate action can be taken to reduce the threats from these risks.

Effective risk management starts by first conducting an assessment (or analysis) to understand the threats and vulnerabilities relevant to your organization, then using the knowledge gained to identify ways to mitigate the risks. Cyber risk (highlighted in Chapter 4) is one area to address: in the world of IT there are many potential threats to be assessed. A threat is any circumstance or event with the potential to cause a loss or danger. In IT this could be categorized as loss of:

▶ confidentiality – a password, market intelligence or a piece of intellectual property

▶ integrity – spam, a virus or hacking into a file or website

▶ continuity – the service is interrupted, e.g. by power outage or by the server going down without a backup.

Clearly, there can be a range of threats, so categorizing them and having a range of alert levels and associated responses will help to ensure that appropriate resource and service levels are allocated to minimize losses or danger. Dividing threats into four categories can help to begin the risk prioritization process:

1 **External threats** – things beyond the control and borders of the organization

2 **Internal threats** – things within the control and borders of the organization

3 **Human threats** – things such as terrorism, burglary, sabotage and arson

4 **Natural threats** – things related to climate (i.e. extreme weather events) or acts of nature (e.g. tsunamis or earthquakes).

Each category, apart from natural threats, can also then be divided into either intentional or accidental. These categories can be used to identify the potential risk, so that possible courses of action and responses can be considered – for example, insurance against type of loss – and steps taken to mitigate the threat.

For example, in a small business with one computer, the owner may decide to have anti-virus software, back up their data to the 'cloud', and have some type of data protection program to mitigate the potential risks. At the other end of the spectrum, the actions that an intensive care unit (ICU) may put in place in a hospital would be far greater, as the potential risks are quite different.

Risk management

▶ Cultural approaches

Different countries also have different approaches to risk management (see Chapter 3). Generally, developing countries tend to be lower in uncertainty avoidance, often because there is still a strong sense of family and community, so if someone takes a risk and it results in financial loss or failure, there is a strong support network around them to help. By contrast, in more developed western societies the trend is to focus more on the individual and less on community and external support.

Caspar Berry, a former professional poker player who is now a speaker on risk and decision-making, admires the approach to risk that Germans seem to take. For example, there are no speed limits on their autobahns, which one might perceive as highly risky. Yet the autobahn fatality rate of 1.7 deaths per billion kilometres travelled compares well with the 5.1 rate on urban streets and the 7.6 rate on rural roads in Germany. While the leading cause of accidents on autobahns is 'excessive speed', the police determine that this means that one party is generally driving too fast for the prevailing weather conditions, which perhaps says more about how human judgement is considered more important than enforcing rules to minimize risk. Berry comments:

> 'In order for people to make better decisions, an understanding of risk in a mathematical way is very important. This does not mean a calculator has to be used every time, because we all have a brilliant,

yet flawed decision-making process which is called gut feel. I think the Germans are good at managing risk because they use both mathematical data and gut feel to make their decisions.'

▶ Phases of risk-taking

Another person who uses a combination of gut feel and logic to make decisions is Professor Hugh Montgomery, UCL Professor of Intensive Care Medicine in London. He is known for his pioneering genetic research into the ACE fitness gene, which determines our capacity for either strength or endurance. Montgomery has also run several 100-km ultra-marathons, taken part in skydiving, holds the world record for underwater piano playing, and has climbed 8,200-metre Cho Oyu with the Xtreme Everest research group. He believes that there are four distinct phases of managing risk during our lifetime, as outlined below.

1st phase – no knowledge of risk (childhood: curiosity)

As we start out on life's journey, we are unaware of any potential risks, and so there is no 'risk-management' activity. In Hugh's case, as a young boy full of curiosity, he decided to put a metal fork in an electrical socket to see what would happen. He was hit with an enormous jolt and saw a flash, which, while scary, was also exciting, so – because his parents were not in the room at the time – he did it again.

You don't have to be young to have this carefree and spontaneous attitude to risk. There are two risk types similarly named in the Risk Type Compass described in Chapter 2, which highlight the desire for excitement and spontaneity.

2nd phase – indestructible (adolescence: robust)

As young people begin to develop some maturity, they often believe that 'it won't happen to me'. As Hugh grew up, he was encouraged to take risks and liked to challenge himself. Consequently, by the age of 15, Hugh was part of the diving team that investigated the treasures of the sunken Tudor ship *Mary Rose*. During his late teens, Hugh discovered an opportunity to be paid £1,500 for being a test volunteer in a medical experiment. The test involved radiation. Hugh's father (a paediatrician) was not keen for him to do this but recognized his son's desire to take risks and that it was his choice. Asked by Hugh for advice, his father said, if Hugh was that desperate to have money, he would give him the £1,500 himself, since he thought that even a small dose of radiation was likely to have implications. Hugh convinced himself that it was not dangerous and went ahead. Today he admits that perhaps he should have made a different decision. On another occasion, he decided to go canoeing in a friend's canoe, which was a bit of a tight fit. He did not worry; he just wedged himself in. Later, when it rolled over and he was upside down in the water, he found he was stuck and could not get out. It was only shallow water, but still very dangerous.

These examples show characteristics of the adventurous type in the Risk Type Compass, where someone is both impulsive and fearless and more likely to be operating on their intuitive gut feel than thinking things through. This can then result in the person managing the implications of a risk once it has happened rather than preparing for it ahead of time.

3rd phase – chess player (working out the moves)

Still enjoying adventurous pursuits such as mountaineering, underwater diving and skydiving in his adult years, Hugh now enjoyed planning his adventures, coming up with different ways to manage potential risks and testing his intellect. Sometimes the tests were more extreme than anticipated. Once, when working as a commercial diver, he was in murky waters inside a submerged ship and found himself stuck in the ship's funnel. This meant that he couldn't go on further or turn round. After quickly thinking through his options and the amount of oxygen he had left, he began wriggling backwards to extract himself, all the time being mindful that over-anxiety would cause him to use up valuable oxygen.

The characteristics of this phase of Hugh's life correlate more with the composed or deliberate risk types, where the person gives much more thought and consideration to the risks of an activity in order to manage any potential hazards or threats.

4th phase – acceptance (recognizing and tolerating limitations)

Now in later life, Hugh is more accepting that bad things can happen and he now views his risk-taking in the broader context of family, community and the world around him. Therefore he aims to balance his life and the risks he takes with the responsibilities and inevitable physical decline he faces. There is also perhaps a change in the areas of risk that he is managing: that is, he is moving from taking physical risks to financial and reputational risks as his career develops.

This stage may correspond with the risk types of deliberate and composed, as described in the Risk Type Compass. His extensive experience of risk-taking earlier in his life has provided a rich database to learn from and, combined with the logical consideration of risks, his behaviour at this stage is based more on wisdom and experience than youthful enthusiasm.

▶ Finding your risk boundaries

These phases identified by Professor Montgomery also correlate with the experience of David Brabham, Australian racing driver and Triple Le Mans 24 Hours class winner.

He describes risk as:

> 'pushing myself and the car to the limit and finding the edge, and then staying there as long as possible. There is a danger to driving, which makes it attractive to me, and I find that I can push the car's boundaries as well as my own and achieve more than I thought was possible.'

▲ David Brabham

Brabham's four phases of risk management started with curiosity to find out whether he could climb the highest trees on the farm where he grew up. He also drove the farm vehicles flat out, making them go sideways for as long as possible to see how far he could travel this way. He acknowledges that everyone has to go through the 'indestructible phase' and he observes this with his son, now also a racing driver:

> 'It's difficult to short-cut gaining experience, and people only learn by going out trying things for themselves and making mistakes. It is no good me telling him what to do, he has to do it, and that is

what is needed for the foundations of a long-term career. I have realized that how I can influence him positively is to have my son around when I work with other drivers, as he is more likely to absorb the advice I give to others than if I was to tell him it directly.

'When you are younger you don't realize where the boundaries lie, and when you push your car to the limit, you normally end up walking back to the pits. Some people are more risk-takers than others, and if they go over the limits they have an accident, but then they understand those boundaries better. But you have to push it to know what's possible.'

▶ Mindset and risk management

David Brabham also believes that mindset is a factor in managing risk, particularly for those who have reached the top of their game. It's very hard to get into Formula 1, he says, and even harder to stay there:

'There are plenty of talented young drivers, but it's not just about talent, it's about money. There is pressure on the race teams to work with both talent and those who have the biggest bank cheque.

'If you are signed as a driver for a year, even after the first race, other drivers are going in your motorhome *and talking about the following year with the team. If you don't block that out, and worry about looking over your shoulder then you will start to make mistakes, and the pressure builds, because others are putting doubts in you. It's a harsh environment and you have to be strong within yourself and not distracted by other people.'*

According to Rebecca Harding, CEO of Delta Economics, another method of managing risk is to ensure that you can filter out the things that don't matter. She believes that, by allowing time and space, a commodity that may be in short supply, you can focus on what is important and relevant in an objective manner:

'I have very little time but what I always do is to leave half an hour between each meeting in London, and walk to the next meeting if I can. I don't put on my phone or respond to calls; I just focus on what has happened, assess it and clear my head. It really enables me to work out what the important things are that I should be paying attention to.'

David Brabham concurs with this view:

'I perform best when my mind is quite still. When it's busy with lots of talking in my head, the fear factor changes, and that's what causes the hurdles ahead. It's not easy to do when you have a lot of outside distractions, but when you do, and you stay in the present, you can suddenly find that you have achieved what you wanted to, despite the potential risks.'

▶ The implications of timescales

It has already been mentioned that timescale is a factor in risk management. People often think too much in the short term and are so risk-averse that they believe their hands are tied and they do not feel empowered to take action. They refuse to countenance thinking differently because of the perceived implications of what might happen if they did.

It's all about timeframe. If you are unable to escape the constraints of short-term thinking, and what might happen if you tried something different and it failed, you will perceive the consequences to be too uncomfortable and painful, despite the potential longer-term benefits. Focusing on the long term is important in managing risk, but it often means changing our mindset.

Caspar Berry believes that it is important that people differentiate between conscious risk-taking and risk that happens to us. He explains that, if your plane crashes or your parachute fails to open, these are risks that happen to us, and there is no long term. But there are certain conscious decisions we can make that can have an impact on the long term. For example, at one end of the spectrum of risk is the immediate risk of rejection that a salesperson faces when they pick up the phone and the person says no. This is because the human psyche is driven to keep us safe and we do not to want to fail. Yet, despite this potential risk, salespeople still make calls because they believe that there will be long-term gains.

Shrewd businesses want their people to make decisions that will bring the greatest chance of return on investment, and they know that that does not mean the highest chance of short-term success. They take a longer-term view of the decisions made, because what is important is their net effect. We don't make a lot of big decisions in our lives every day. The only way to judge our decision-making ability is to take a longitudinal perspective – that is, assess the quality of the decisions we make over time.

'People judge themselves on their decisions today, and you have to extract yourself from the pain of that moment and focus on the longer-term journey.'

Caspar Berry

People often don't want to wait for the long term but Caspar Berry believes that it is a form of incompetence to base decisions only on short-term results. He points out that record companies used to wait five years for a musician to get a hit record, and some of the most successful managers of sports teams did not win anything for around five years.

'I believe that part of risk management and judgement is to know where you are going to invest your

▲ Thinking in the long term is important in risk management

resources, but also giving those good investments time. It is part of leadership and it's standing by your beliefs. In the late 1990s when tech stocks went through the roof, Warren Buffett [most successful investor in the 20th century] stood by his beliefs. That's what judgement is and that is what leadership is.'

Long-term thinking means being concerned with what your industry or sector might look like in the future. The energy company Shell has a Scenarios team that looks ahead to 2050 and tries to work out what future energy demands might mean in terms of risk. They ask a series of 'What if?' questions to force thinking about the future in order to help the company prepare to respond and act now.

▶ Trust and risk management

It is not uncommon for people to inadvertently assume that their view on risk is shared by others and will be treated the same way. Why is this? Simply stated, it is because risk is relative – relative to other people's character, disposition, state, experience and perspective.

Think about being a passenger in a car and then being the driver of the car. Most people can begin to notice a difference in terms of risk management. When you are not at the controls, you leave the management of risk to the driver.

In the business world, a CEO has to trust his or her team to manage risks, but that trust is not always reciprocated. In large corporations, employees rarely know much about senior business leaders, let alone admire them, and yet both parties need to trust one another. In a vehicle driver's case, they trust that the passenger will not interfere. With business leaders, should they demonstrate trust first or expect that others will trust them immediately?

This principle of trust is at the heart of Google's culture. There is a mutual relationship of transparency and sharing, based on the belief that, if you give people control, they will use it. So, from a risk-management perspective, trust is also a key component.

Being positive about risk-taking

Organizations are often more focused on problem solving than on recognizing and celebrating their achievements. How risky would it be for business leaders and managers as well as politicians and media executives to consider introducing **eustress** into their work environments and aim to minimize distress?

Eustress is the good stress that motivates you to continue working. It can provide the incentive to get the job done. It refers to the positive response you have to a stressor. When you engage in a challenge or an activity that excites you, and that you know will take you slightly 'out of your comfort zone', that is eustress. Examples include watching a scary film or playing a competitive sport you enjoy. Everyone can benefit from some stress in his or her work in order to continue to be happy, motivated, challenged and productive. It is when this stress is no longer tolerable and/or manageable that **distress** comes in.

A component of stress is the timeframe given to it and it often means that people are thinking too much in the short term. Part of risk management is about good judgement and about knowing where you are going to focus your resources and giving those good investments time. The greatest returns on investment are not necessarily gained by the opportunity most likely to succeed in the short term. Most people don't want to fail, so they find themselves focusing on things that are most likely to succeed immediately, but this is not necessarily the best way to manage risk for the long term.

▶ Risk management and people

Perhaps one of the biggest risks that an organization takes is in the recruitment of people. To minimize the risk of not attracting top talent, a global corporation needs to focus on:

▶ providing the traditional 'hygiene factors' such as appropriate working environment, recognition and fair pay

▶ offering continuing professional development (CPD) so that employees can further develop their skills

▶ offering opportunities for international mobility

▶ being in the lists of top employers (e.g. *The Times's* Top 100 Graduate Employers).

The media have a significant influence on graduate expectations, and there is a risk that, if a company does not fulfil these expectations, it won't be able to employ the brightest talent for the future. As discussed in Chapter 4, the young people of the millennial generation tend to be more interested in a company's values and how it treats its people compared to previous generations, as well as whether the business has a social conscience.

With more senior-level hires, another risk for employers to manage is to consider broader issues surrounding the proposition, not only from the perspective of the person being hired but also their spouse, particularly if international work is likely. Can the spouse get a job easily, or is there an opportunity for retraining? The individual is seen now as part of a bigger system (the family) and therefore family safety and the happiness of the spouse and children have an influence on the emotions of the employee too.

The culture within some consultancy firms such as McKinsey is to keep in touch with an employee even when they leave the company, because they are viewed as part of the alumni. While this might seem onerous, it is a shrewd method of risk management, because it provides a route for referrals and leaves the door open for individuals potentially to return at some time in the future.

Human resources departments within organizations are now focused on developing resilience as a method of risk management. Because of the pace of change in many large firms, the ability to be resilient is a skill that employees now require. These changes may come in the form of managing work–life balance, working virtually and coping with unexpected situations. What is involved in managing risk now is extremely wide-ranging in large organizations and not just the remit of one department.

Summary

This chapter has explored how different people use different approaches to risk management, with practical examples, and what some of the issues are for individuals and organizations in order for them to be aware of the wide-ranging nature of risks. In the next chapter we will consider the future of risk and how society as a whole may have to pay attention to these key issues.

6

Risk and the future

'Risk management can be a powerful instrument for development – not only by building people's resilience and thus reducing the effects of adverse events but also by allowing them to take advantage of opportunities for improvement.'

World Development Report 2014, *'Risk and Opportunity'*

Having outlined what risk is and how it is defined and managed, we now explore how risk might affect us in the future as the world changes. No matter where you are in the world, over the last 25 years or so there has been unprecedented change. There has been economic reform, democratic participation, technological advancements, and improvements in health and developments in science. For some, this has meant escaping poverty and deprivation, for others an improvement in living standards and educational opportunities. And within all these changes lies a degree of risk. It is likely that the speed of these changes is only likely to increase, and therefore being able to anticipate and manage risk will be a key factor in how society addresses these changes.

The World Development Report of 2014 suggests that countries and people need to be better prepared to cope with both adverse and positive events, as well as being able to assess the obstacles that they might face, which could include information availability, incentives and constraints on resources, and how groups and collective action can play their part.

▶ Collaborative working

The importance of collaboration and co-ordination is not to be underestimated, and it is a view also shared by the leaders of the World Economic Forum in their *Global Risks* report of 2014. Because the world is so interconnected now, more than ever before, what happens in one geography or economy is likely to have consequences in another. A recent example is how quickly the US sub-prime mortgage crisis triggered the recession of 2008 and affected the whole world economy, particularly in Europe where many of the banks then used taxpayer money to bail out their ailing banking systems which had been damaged by the so-called 'toxic loans' on their balance sheets.

The World Economic Forum lists the top ten global risks of highest concern in 2014 as follows:

1 Fiscal crises in key economies

2 Structurally high unemployment/underemployment

3 Water crises

4 Severe income disparity

5 Failure of climate change mitigation and adaptation

6 Greater incidence of extreme weather events, such as floods

7 Global governance failure

8 Food crises

9 Failure of major financial mechanism/institution

10 Profound political and social instability.

The Forum believes that a co-ordinated approach to addressing these issues is paramount, particularly in relation to the macro-economic ones where the impact of one is highly interconnected with the others. The report also identifies three other factors that are likely to have a strong influence on the interdependencies and interconnections of these risks:

▶ **Today's generation** – graduates coming out of higher education with significant debts, facing high unemployment and the likelihood of not fulfilling their economic potential in the short term, which can lead to social unrest.

▶ **Instability,** with a focus on local – with changes in demographics and greater financial burdens on governments, there are increased pressures for more of a domestic focus on economic and energy security rather than a co-ordinated global perspective. Developing economies face short-term pressure to focus on rapid economic growth, which means that they pay less attention to longer-term global issues.

▶ **Cyber attacks** – as the planet increasingly relies on being interconnected in the digital world, the risk of future challenges and attacks in cyberspace would have a global impact.

All in all, this means that it is likely to become increasingly difficult for agreement to be reached on issues with a global impact because there are so many other big issues for countries to address. One global area that is particularly relevant is climate change, listed as the fifth highest global risk in the above report.

▶ Communication of risk

A recently published report by the University College London (UCL) Policy Commission on communicating climate science recognized that if the messages about climate change are to be listened to, accepted and acted upon in the future, it is vital that climate scientists communicate in a different way with the general public than previously (Rapley *et al.*, 2014). The report concurs with the research, described in Chapter 2, showing how neuroscience and psychology have an impact on how people receive and analyse information. This means that, if scientists are not aware of how their communication is received by the general public, they are unlikely to be as effective as they might wish to be.

Because our brain is hardwired to keep us safe, it assigns 'meaning in context' to information that it receives, based on our previous experiences as well as on cultural and social factors. This means that, if two different people who could both be described as intelligent read the same facts about climate change, they could arrive at different viewpoints, based on how their brains assimilate and interpret the information. This is because our higher cognition, described as System 1 and System 2 thinking (see Chapter 2), readily accepts thinking that supports our previous beliefs but subjects disconfirming evidence to critical examination.

Daniel Kahneman's research showed that System 1 is the faster, intuitive thinking that operates outside our conscious awareness, and System 2, the reflective reasoning, is more effortful and slower, and in many cases used to rationalize intuitions rather than analyse them in a sensible manner. What this means for scientists is that just communicating more facts about climate change is not the answer – it is *how* these facts are communicated that is important. Scientists therefore need to determine the social and cultural values and the context around which the information is provided. This relates to the cultural theory of risk (see Chapter 2) and how our values shape our approach to risk on any given issue.

In July 2014, neuroscientists from the Institute of Cognitive Neuroscience at University College London wrote in the journal *PNAS* suggesting that an area of the brain, the habenula, which is smaller than a pea, may help us in risky situations since it plays a key role in how we predict, learn and respond to anxiety situations. So, depending on how the facts on climate change are presented, information can provoke feelings and behaviour ranging from fear and despair to avoidance or rejection of the issues, and often rejection of the person presenting them.

▶ Cognitive dissonance

When there is a discrepancy between someone's behaviour and their attitude (such as how could I, a good person, do something that may ultimately negatively impact on others?), it results in what is known as cognitive dissonance. This is where two contradictory beliefs are held at the same time, or where a person is confronted with new information that challenges their existing beliefs, ideas or values.

An example of this might be a person who views themselves as environmentally friendly but who then purchases a car that is not fuel-efficient. What happens is that the person has to take action to reduce the discomfort, so what they could do to is decide to use the car only for long journeys and to take public transport more often for shorter journeys. They would also be likely to avoid situations or information that would prolong the dissonance. In another example, also related to climate change, one might argue that individuals and companies that engage in 'carbon offsetting' are also using it as a way of reducing cognitive dissonance.

▶ Minimizing uncertainty

Another factor in the communication of risk around climate change is the question of uncertainty. Generally, scientists are trained to define and communicate uncertainty along with their findings, which can be interpreted by the general public as doubt. If scientists in this case want individuals to take action to reduce the global risks of climate change, they need to minimize uncertainty in the mind of the individual – something scientists are not currently trained to do.

'An unrelenting emphasis on uncertainty is interpreted by non-scientists as revealing confusion – that less is known about an issue than is actually the case.'

Report of the UCL Policy Commission on Communicating Climate Science, 2014

It is not just scientists who are starting to pay attention to how they communicate potential risks. A UK House of Commons Science and Technology Select Committee report, 'Communicating climate science', recently stated:

> 'A lack of clear, consistent messages on the science has a detrimental impact on the public's trust in climate science. The Government and other bodies are currently failing to make use of social media to engage with the public and to become an authoritative source of accurate scientific information about climate change. Government must work with the learned societies, national academies and other experts to develop a source of information on climate science that is discrete from policy delivery, comprehensible to the general public, and responsive to both current developments and uncertainties in the science.'

▶ Risk and health

Health and well-being are another aspect of society today that can be affected by risk. A World Health Organization report states that over one-third of the world's deaths can be attributed to a small number of risk factors that include high blood pressure, tobacco use, high blood glucose, inactivity and obesity.

The changing picture of health risks depends on what part of the world you live in. In developed countries, populations are living longer, partly because of successes in medicine such as the defeat of infectious diseases. But with increasing incomes and greater sense of 'comfort', people are suffering more from a lack of physical activity and an increase in tobacco and alcohol consumption.

In developing countries, health risks still relate to under-nutrition, lack of clean drinking water, unsafe sex, and poor sanitation and hygiene. These countries are also starting to see an increase in non-communicable diseases such as cancer and cardiovascular disease, which is a double burden for them.

'Worldwide, overweight and obesity cause more deaths than being underweight. The combined burden of these diet-related risks and physical inactivity in low- and middle-income countries is similar to that caused by HIV/AIDS and tuberculosis.'

World Health Organization

While the picture may appear gloomy, technology is beginning to have a major impact on how individuals can take responsibility for managing their health. One way is through 'gamification', which is the use of game thinking to solve problems in non-game contexts. Gamification taps into the primary motivators that influence human behaviour, a subject that has been touched on in many of the chapters in this book, and uses digital game design and game thinking to introduce competition, reward, problem solving and fun to managing health. Elements include goal setting, real-time feedback, levels and badges to show progress and accomplishment, plus the ability to share your data with others. The millennial generation (18–34-year-olds) has been brought up on technology with their smartphones and tablets, so it is something they are very familiar with. Companies are developing a variety of wearable devices such as the Up® Band and Nike Fuel that provide the user with data about their physical activity, diet and sleep.

While currently the data these devices generate can serve to motivate individuals, it is likely that, in the not too distant future, the data generated could play a role in influencing the cost of an insurance policy, with employers being the conduit between the insurance company and the individual. This is happening already in the USA, where health insurance company Cigna launched a pilot programme with one of its corporate customers and distributed free armband devices. According to Cigna, 'early results showed a number of employees on the verge of contracting diabetes have improved their risk profiles'. BP also provided wearable devices to 14,000 of its employees with the incentive that, if the sum total of steps they each walked in 2013 topped one million, they gained points that could go towards a lower insurance premium.

Information from healthcare devices can also be useful to doctors and health professionals in providing early warning of potential risks with patients, both pre- and post-treatment, and it also begins to shift the responsibility away from costly medical facilities on to individuals. While governments are recovering from the financial challenge caused by the economic downturn and have to cope with an increasingly ageing population in many countries, the use of technology in the healthcare sector might be one useful way to spread the responsibility for managing health risks to a broader spectrum of people.

▶ Large-scale behaviour change

While it might seem like a great idea to share your personal health data with your doctor or employer, trust is an important element of managing health risks. Professor Hugh Montgomery, Director at the UCL Institute for Human Health and Performance, believes that three areas need to be addressed when encouraging large-scale attitude and behaviour change in health education. The requirements are:

▶ providing a continuous message

▶ delivery of the message by a trusted vector

▶ gaining emotional buy-in.

His views correspond to those of Nedra Weinreich, an expert in the field of social marketing, who suggests that, to help people change behaviour,

> *'there needs to be a mix of education, where rational facts are used to change their behaviours, and coercion, which forces people to adopt a behaviour under threat of penalty for not doing so. In between those two points lies social marketing – the use of commercial marketing methods to persuade people to change their behaviours for reasons that go beyond the rational facts to appeal to their core values. Often people know exactly what they should be doing and why, and they still disregard what their head tells them. Social marketing utilizes emotional appeals to resonate with the part of the brain that determines what people actually do, as opposed to what they know they should do.'*

Unilever and social marketing

One example of social marketing in practice is the work of Unilever – through its Lifebuoy® soap brand – to influence healthier hygiene habits by changing the hand-washing behaviour of over 1 billion people in Asia, Africa and Latin America by 2015. Their continuous message is focused on washing hands after visiting the toilet and before handling food. The Lifebuoy® brand itself has been around since 1894 and therefore has a high degree of trust among its users, and the campaign is aimed at creating emotional buy-in and not just providing the logical facts.

In India the approach has been simple: to get the message across using bread! Unilever used the gathering of Kumbh Mela in 2013 to spread the message to more than 100 million people who came together to eat, pray and live together. They created a brand stamp with the words 'Did you wash your hands with Lifebuoy®?' and used it on 2.5 million rotis (Indian bread) to encourage millions of people to wash their hands before eating and help stop the spread of preventable diseases including diarrhoea and pneumonia.

▲ Getting the message across

▶ Reliability of information

The Lifebuoy story demonstrates how important the source of the information is in terms of how much it is trusted. And trusted sources will continue to become an even more important commodity in the future when we have to assess and manage risk. This ranges from the public information provided by governments and institutions to the feedback and comments from your friends and acquaintances on social media websites such as Facebook or Twitter.

In Chapter 1 it was highlighted how we assess risk based on:

▶ the available options

▶ the outcomes we value

▶ beliefs about what might follow if we choose each option.

Trusted sources become relevant in influencing our beliefs about what might happen, as they enable us to have a method of short-cutting the mass of information available to us via the Internet. For example, if you want to reduce the potential risk of having a bad experience at a restaurant or in a hotel, many people use websites such as Trip Advisor or Yelp as their trusted source of information.

Even in the field of healthcare, many people do not trust their doctors entirely and are relying more on the Internet for information. A US survey carried out in 2011 showed that 86 per cent of women said they made the decisions about healthcare treatments for all their family members and, while they still trusted their doctor, they went online before and after a consultation to learn more about their diagnosis and prescribed treatments.

In financial services, it has already been mentioned (see Chapter 4) that the reputation of many large banks and financial institutions was dented following the financial meltdown in 2008 resulting in a loss of trust. This matters on a global scale, because a lack of trust in banks could be a factor in the speed of global economic recovery. Mark Carney, the Governor of the Bank of England, warned in 2013 that 'regulatory reforms would prove insufficient in rebuilding public confidence unless they were accompanied by cultural change'.

Professor Roger Steare, Corporate Philosopher in Residence at Cass Business School in London, has been researching the field of values and ethics for a number of years. He has developed the MoralDNA™ profiling tool that measures how people prefer to make moral decisions and what moral values they prefer when doing so. Using this tool, he carried out research on how managers behave at work, and the findings showed that managers become more robotic and less caring at work. It also highlighted a gender divide in terms of ethical preferences: women score 5 per cent higher on the ethic of care at work. Steare believes that too much compliance – rules, laws, regulations and red tape – in business has a tendency to remove personal responsibility from managers for deciding what's right. This suggests that one way to rebuild trust within organizations might be to create the conditions in which managers can act ethically, according to their judgement, rather than removing the element of humanness from the equation.

▶ Interstate conflict

While we may feel as individuals that we can operate in a type of personal vacuum to minimize our risks, the interconnectedness of global society nowadays will undoubtedly continue to have an impact on everyone. Business and governments can be affected by what happens in another part of the world and, with more low-level conflicts happening, this area of risk is only likely to increase. For example, the Russian–Ukraine gas dispute that began in 2005 affected far more countries that just those two. Numerous European countries are reliant on Russian natural gas imports that are shipped through the Ukrainian pipeline, and therefore they had to assess and manage the associated risks of potential conflict and disagreement.

▶ The rise of emerging economies

The BRIC countries (Brazil, Russia, India and China) are now ranked among the top ten economies worldwide. As they grow, they, and other emerging countries such as South Africa, Mexico and Indonesia, offer opportunities for companies prepared to invest in, or export to, these places. However, the rising middle classes can become discontented: they want better services, infrastructure and greater accountability of public officials. This can bring uncertainty and a degree of risk to would-be investors in those countries.

These risks are then quantified by companies such as Maplecroft, founded by Alyson Warhurst, which provide global risk analytics, research and strategic forecasting to governments, global multinationals and institutions. Their data-mapping tools provide analysis of risks at local, country, issue and sector level, and they can help organizations identify, forecast, monitor and manage potential risks to their operations and supply chains.

▶ Data mapping to identify risks

One example of how data can help shape future thinking is when Maplecroft was asked by the global logistics providers to map the potential risks in Africa over the next five to ten years. What one might have expected to be on the list were health, safety, pollution and emissions, but instead what was identified as a major risk was HIV/ Aids, from truck drivers and the communities through which they passed.

The initial reaction of the logistics companies was to suggest that it was the responsibility of governments to deal with this problem. After Maplecroft did more research that confirmed this as a major issue, they spoke to logistics managers in the different countries, who confirmed that their biggest problem was the reliability of drivers: while business was booming, the managers were not always in a position to fulfil demand due to lack of resource. So it seemed that the effects of HIV/Aids posed an enormous risk for any company looking to either import to or export from Africa.

The logistics companies then started to work with the World Food Programme to set up mobile health centres for truck drivers. Because continuity of treatment was one of the biggest challenges, the oil and gas companies that needed to get their products out of Africa developed a road map with the major truck routes on one side and the location of the health centres on the other. They also worked with Nike and the Nike Foundation to find ways to help adolescent girls protect themselves from HIV. This meant that, from risk mapping, the logistics companies moved to risk resilience and addressed risks that might not have been spotted otherwise.

▶ Risk blindness

As the example above shows, sometimes risks are not identified until you look at data or consider a situation from a new perspective. This book aims to provide this different perspective on the subject of risk and in this context it is useful to consider the question of risk blindness. This is when something changes so slowly or happens so infrequently that we think it is never going to happen. A turkey could happily assume that it will be well fed every day, until along comes Christmas or Thanksgiving; it does not realize that this particular infrequent event in the year is going to have fatal consequences.

People still live happily in San Francisco, even though it is on the San Andreas fault line, which means a high risk of earthquakes. Adventurers still visit the Arctic in spring even though they know that polar bears are often hungry when they come out of hibernation. In business, some companies refuse to invest in new technology to improve or adapt their product because they have been in business for 20 years and have never had a credible competitor. Investing in technology would mean a dent in their short-term profits, which they have got used to, or they have pressure to deliver short-term profits to meet investors' expectations.

People get so used to the familiarity around them that they become blind to the potential risks, or sometimes they see them but choose to overlook them. This is known as **wilful blindness**.

In her book on the subject, Margaret Heffernan offers some examples of when people have been blind to the evidence that proves they are wrong. She recounts the story of Alice Stewart, who began work as a resident physician in Oxford in 1941. As she developed her career, Alice began to try and find answers to the question of why so many children aged between two and four years old were developing leukaemia. With little money for research, she worked long hours and eventually realized that the common denominator was that three out of four mothers of affected children had been given an obstetric X-ray during pregnancy. Alice Stewart's research, first published in 1958, concluded that a foetus exposed to an X-ray was twice as likely to develop cancer within ten years as a foetus that had not been exposed. However, it was not until 1980 that major US medical organizations finally recommended that the practice be stopped.

Why did it take so long to address this risk? There were several reasons but perhaps the main one was that Alice's research challenged the big idea that was central to scientific thinking at the time. Doctors had become blind to the obvious. In order to address risk blindness or wilful blindness, we need to acknowledge our biases and recognize that they influence how we look at the world, and how we consider risk. In business it can also be beneficial to have someone whose role it is to challenge and to question, and who is not part of the 'organizational system'. However, playing the role of sceptic can be difficult because it can make others in the organization feel uncomfortable. They may close ranks to dismiss the challenges or questions and view the sceptic as an 'outsider'.

Summary

In order to cope effectively and manage risks in future, it is worth remembering the following key points:

We evaluate risks and make decisions all the time. The key is to review the quality of those decisions and their longer-term impact. It might sound ridiculous, but the more decisions you make, the better you become at making them. Take time to write them down, review them and reflect on whether you can trust your judgement.

Risk can be minimized but not eliminated. If we eliminated all risks, we would in effect be stagnating, as the world changes around us.

Making decisions around risk is based on logic, emotion, external information and previous experience. We can develop an intuitive sense of an outcome that can be totally unjustified, when based on the facts. To broaden your perspective, access multiple sources of information, but remember that it will probably be incomplete and inaccurate.

Bring more breadth and depth to how you assess risk. All risks have an upside and a potential downside, so consider both before making your decisions.

Expect failure. Part of being able to practise risk-taking is experiencing failure, so view it as part of the learning process, not the end result.

Take the long-term view. In terms of risk-taking, go for the long-term view. There is so much evidence to show that rarely does anyone become an overnight success. They have been taking risks, practising and learning for many years. By applying the other points above, you can become better at identifying, evaluating, analysing and managing risk.

This 100 ideas section gives you ways you can explore the subject in more depth. It is much more than just the usual reading list.

100 IDEAS

Ten risky things to do

1 Stop watching TV for one week.

2 Say no when someone asks for your help, with no explanation.

3 Cry in public.

4 Learn something new.

5 Go and visit the one place in the world you have always wanted to see.

6 Speak to a stranger.

7 Forgive someone you have had an argument with.

8 Read a book on a subject that you think is of no interest to you.

9   Ask your boss for a pay rise.

10   Try an extreme sport that you have not done before.

Ten risk-takers

11   Philippe Petit – high-wire artist

This man has done some amazing high-wire walks over the Sydney Harbour Bridge, Notre Dame Cathedral and between the Twin Towers of the World Trade Center.

12   Meredith Whitney – bank analyst

Meredith Whitney was recognized as one of Wall Street's most controversial research analysts, and among the first to recognize the sub-prime mortgage crisis. In 2007 she made a pessimistic, but accurate, report on Citigroup. Later that year Forbes.com named her as the second-best stock picker in the capital-market industry.

13   Sherron Watkins – whistleblower at Enron

Watkins had been Vice-President of Corporate Development at the Enron Corporation. In August 2001, she alerted the CEO of Enron at that time, Kenneth Lay, of accounting irregularities in financial reports, which eventually led to the collapse of the firm.

14   Jamsetji Nusserwanji Tata – founder of the Tata Group, India

Tata was founder of India's largest conglomerate group. Born in 1839, he was brought up in a family of priests, and broke tradition to become the first member of the family to go into business. He devoted his life to four goals: setting up an iron and steel company, creating a world-class learning institution, and building a unique hotel and a hydroelectric plant. Only the hotel was built in his lifetime, with the other three ideas being achieved by his successors.

15 Victor Boyarsky – Russian polar scientist and explorer

Boyarsky worked as a polar scientist for the Arctic and Antarctic Research Institute in Saint Petersburg from 1973 to 1987. During that time he took part in polar expeditions. In 1988 he became a member of an international expedition, traversing from the south to the north of Greenland on dog sleds and skis. A year later he was a member of the International Transantarctic Expedition, which used dog sleds and took more than seven months, the longest crossing of Antarctica in history.

16 Bill Stone – US explorer and daredevil caver

He has explored some of the deepest caves on earth, including some that are more than 1,370 metres (4,500 feet) underground.

17 Dick Smith – Australian entrepreneur and aviator

Entrepreneur Dick Smith founded Dick Smith Electronics in 1968 as a small car radio installation business and sold it to Woolworths in 1982 for $20 million. Smith learned to fly in 1972 and in 1982–3 he successfully completed the first solo helicopter flight around the world.

18 Brene Brown – American researcher, author and speaker

Currently a research professor at the University of Houston Graduate College of Social Work, Brown shot to fame as a result of her TED talk on the subject of vulnerability, which has now been watched by over 6 million people worldwide. Her research highlighted that the shaming culture we live in makes it harder than ever to show courage and be vulnerable – in other words, to take a risk.

19 Rosa Parks – African-American civil rights activist

On 1 December 1955 Rosa Parks refused to obey bus driver James F. Blake's order to give up her seat in the colored section to a white passenger, after the white section was filled. Her act of defiance is an important symbol of the modern civil rights movement.

20 Malala Yousafzai – stood up to the Taliban

In 2012 Malala Yousafzai was a 15-year-old student in the Swat region of Pakistan who voiced her disagreement when the Taliban forbade education for girls. In response, the Taliban stopped the school bus she was on and shot her in the head. Malala survived and went on to become a symbol for change because she risked her life to raise awareness of the issue that a disproportionate number of girls had no access to education.

Ten risky places to visit

21 Burj Khalifa in Dubai, UAE

If you are afraid of heights, this is probably not the best place to visit. At 828 metres (2,717 feet) high, it is currently the tallest building in the world.

22 Sichuan–Tibet Highway, China

Frequent hazards such as avalanches, rock slides and poor weather on this road result in 7,500 deaths for every 100,000 drivers using it.

23 Tokyo-Yokohama, Japan

Named as one of the world's riskiest cities, its 37 million inhabitants regularly face threats of floods, tsunami, earthquakes and monsoons. The Great Kanto Earthquake of 1923 devastated both Tokyo and Yokohama, killing an estimated 142,800 people.

24 Mount Everest

The highest mountain in the world is over 8,848 metres (29,000 feet) high, but you can visit base camp on the south side in Nepal, which is at an altitude of 5,364 metres (17,598 feet) and one of the most popular trekking routes in the Himalayas.

25 The Strip in Las Vegas, Nevada

If you like gambling, there are numerous casinos on the strip in Las Vegas. In 2012, according to the Nevada Gaming Commission, the 42 casinos they define as being on the Strip had combined revenue of $6,207 billion dollars.

26 The Dubai Mall, UAE

If you like shopping, it might take you a while to get round the world's biggest shopping mall. It contains over 1,200 shops and has 502,000 square metres (5,403,000 square feet) of retail space, not to mention over 14,000 car parking spaces.

27 Namaqua National Park, South Africa

This national park, home to the world's largest concentration of succulent plants and situated about 495 km (308 miles) north of Cape Town, is a risky place to visit if you have allergies: it is a biodiversity 'hotspot'. During most of the year few flowers can be seen, but in August and September, after the rains, wild flowers bloom over hundreds of kilometres.

28 Atacama Desert, Northern Chile

The Atacama Desert is a 1,000-km (1,600-mile) strip of land between Peru's southern border and the north of Chile. It is the world's driest place, with average rainfall of 15 mm (0.59 inches) per year.

29 Outer space

Only 536 people from 38 countries have so far gone into space. Of the 536, three people completed only a sub-orbital flight, 533 people reached Earth orbit, 24 travelled beyond low Earth orbit and 12 walked on the moon.

30 Pinnacles National Park, California, USA

If you don't like getting stung by bees, then perhaps this is a place to avoid. Pinnacles National Park has the highest known bee diversity of any place on Earth. The bees range in colour from black, bronze, blue, brown to metallic green, and the regular striped yellow and black.

Ten quotes about risk

31 'If you don't read the newspaper, you're uninformed. If you read the newspaper, you're misinformed.' – Mark Twain

32 'Only those who will risk going too far can possibly find out how far one can go.' – T. S. Eliot

33 'Yes, risk-taking is inherently failure-prone. Otherwise, it would be called sure-thing-taking.' – Jim McMahon

34 'People who don't take risks generally make about two big mistakes a year. People who do take risks generally make about two big mistakes a year.' – Peter F. Drucker

35 'An adventure is only an inconvenience rightly considered. An inconvenience is only an adventure wrongly considered.' – G. K. Chesterton

36 'I am always doing that which I cannot do, in order that I may learn how to do it.' – Pablo Picasso

37 'The fishermen know that the sea is dangerous and the storm terrible, but they have never found these dangers sufficient reason for remaining ashore.' – Vincent van Gogh

38 'The most important thing to remember is this: to be ready at any moment to give up what you are for what you might become.' – W. E. B. Du Bois

39 'Behold the turtle. He makes progress only when he sticks his neck out.' – James B. Conant

40 'Hesitation increases in relation to risk in equal proportion to age.' – Ernest Hemingway

Ten organizations related to risk

41   The World Resources Institute

WRI is a global research organization that works closely with leaders to turn big ideas into action to sustain a healthy environment. www.wri.org

42   The Institute of Risk Management

Founded in 1986, IRM is the leading professional body for risk management, to meet the demand for qualifications in risk management. It is a not-for-profit organization that champions excellence in managing risk. www.theirm.org

43   The Health and Safety Executive

The mission of this government organization is to prevent death, injury and ill health in UK workplaces. www.hse.gov.uk

44   The US Food and Drug Administration

This US federal agency aims to protect and promote public health. It is responsible for assuring the efficacy and security of human and veterinary drugs, biological products, medical devices, food supply, cosmetics, and products that emit radiation. www.fda.gov

45   The International Institute of Risk and Safety Management

IIRSM was established in 1975 as a professional body for health and safety practitioners. It was created to advance professional standards in accident prevention and occupational health throughout the world. www.iirsm.org

46   The Global Risk Institute in Financial Services

Founded by public and private sectors in Canada, GRI's mission is to develop applied and integrative research in financial risk and to enhance risk education for organizations around the world. http://globalriskinstitute.org

47 **The Risk Management Institution of Australasia**

RMIA is the largest professional association of risk management professionals in the Asia–Pacific region. It has over 30 years' experience in representing the practice of risk management. www.rmia.org.au

48 **Maplecroft**

Maplecroft is the world's leading global risk analytics, research and strategic forecasting company. It provides country risk analysis, interactive maps and risk indices. www.maplecroft.com

49 **Delta Economics**

Delta Economics forecasts trade competitiveness, trade payments and has the only trade-based model of GDP in the world. Their forecasts enable businesses to make decisions and cover 200 countries and trade corridors across 10,000 commodity groups. www.deltaeconomics.com

50 **The World Future Society**

The World Future Society is an organization of people dedicated to exploring the future. Their mission is to enable thinkers, political personalities, scientists and laypeople to share an informed, serious dialogue on what the future will be like. www.wfs.org

Ten risky movies

51 *Risky Business* (1983)

Starring Tom Cruise and Rebecca De Mornay, this film is about a normally well-behaved teenager who is looking for an element of risk while his parents are away, but the situation quickly gets out of hand.

52 *Risk* (2007)

This Bollywood film directed by Vishram Sawant stars Randeep Hooda, who plays a policeman fighting the Mumbai criminal underworld.

53 *Rush* (2013)

Ron Howard directed this film, starring James Emsworth and Daniel Bruhl, which highlights the 1970s rivalry between James Hunt and Niki Lauda on the racetrack.

54 *Risk* (2000)

Starring Bryan Brown and Tom Long, this film is about a naive insurance adjuster who is led astray by his jaded boss and gets caught in a web of deceit and lust.

55 *Maximum Risk* (1996)

A policeman attends a murder scene and finds out that the victim was the twin brother he did not know existed. He takes his brother's place and inherits his problems, and his girlfriend. Starring Jean-Claude Van Damme and Natasha Henstridge.

56 *The Risk* (1960) (Original title: *Suspect*)

A British thriller by the Boulting brothers starring Tony Britton and Virginia Maskell.

57 *The Beautiful Risk* (2013) (Original title: *Le beau risqué*)

William (played by Shaun Benson) is a respected artist who loses everything in his divorce. He arrives in Montreal for a job, but it falls through, and he forms a relationship with a woman named Paulette.

58 *The Gift: At Risk* (2007) (Original title: *The Gift: Life Unwrapped*)

Starring Vince Vaughn and Elaine Krausz, the film combines modern technology with romantic tragedy.

59 *Captain Phillips* (2013)

Starring Tom Hanks, this film tells the true story of the hijacking of the MV *Maersk Alabama*, the first US cargo ship to be hijacked in 200 years.

60 *Apollo 13* (1995)

This film, starring Tom Hanks, Bill Paxton and Kevin Bacon, chronicles the risky story of three astronauts who must devise a strategy to return to Earth after their spacecraft is damaged.

Ten risky careers

61 Stuntman

62 Alaskan deep-sea fisherman

63 Lion tamer

64 E-waste recycler

65 Bodyguard

66 Firefighter

67 Search-and-rescue pilot

68 Land mine remover

69 Farmer

70 Commercial diver

Ten areas of risk

71   **Financial risk:** the probability of losing money and not gaining an adequate financial return

72   **Ethical risk:** the consequences of unethical behaviour, i.e. lack of integrity, personal dishonesty, anti-competitive practices

73   **Health and safety risk:** the likelihood that a person may be harmed or suffer adversely if exposed to a hazard

74   **Social risk:** concern or uncertainty in a buyer's mind that the purchase of a product under consideration will not be approved of by others

75   **Recreational risk:** the possibility of a hazard that could lead to a loss, while carrying out a recreational activity

76   **Environmental risk:** actual or potential threat of adverse effects on living organisms and the environment by effluents, emissions, wastes, resource depletion, arising out of an organization's activities

77   **Friendship risk:** the risk of losing a friendship by telling the truth or carrying out an action that you believe may challenge the nature of the relationship

78   **Credit risk:** the risk that a company or individual will be unable to pay the contractual interest or principal on its debt obligations

79   **Industry risk:** the risks affecting a particular industry, e.g. shortages of raw materials or changes in consumer preferences

80   **Business risk:** the possibility that a company will have lower than anticipated profits, or that it will experience a loss rather than a profit.

Ten interesting probabilities

81 The odds of being hit by lightning in the US in any one year are 1 in 700,000.

82 The chance of winning the jackpot in the UK National Lottery is 1 in 14 million.

83 There is a 1 in 6 chance of dying from heart disease.

84 The odds of dying in a plane crash are 1 in 11 million.

85 For mothers who have already given birth to twins, their chances of conceiving another set are about 1 in 14.

86 In the UK, a girl born in 2011 has a 1 in 3 chance of living to their 100th birthday, and a boy has a 1 in 4 chance.

87 A baby born in Sierra Leone is three and a half times more likely to die before its fifth birthday than a child born in India, and more than a hundred times more likely to die than a child born in Iceland or Singapore.

88 The odds of winning an Olympic medal are 662,000 to 1.

89 In any football match, the favourite team wins only 55 per cent of the time.

90 In the US, the odds of becoming a billionaire are 1 in 7,000,000.

Ten future risks and opportunities

91 **Pandemics** – Globalization has created the conditions that could propel viruses around the world. As they become more sophisticated and resistant to modern drugs, how does society address this issue?

92 **Ageing** – How well will society cope with people living to over 100 years old?

93 Technology – Advances in healthcare, cars, retail and many other areas will change how we live our lives.

94 Megacities – Megacities can be defined as having a population over 10 million people, and currently there are 24 on the planet. By 2029 it is expected there will be 29, which may bring challenges in relation to pollution, energy requirements and healthcare.

95 Obesity – Obesity is second only to tobacco in the number of deaths it causes each year in the USA, among adults under the age of 70, and it's not the only country facing this issue. What risks does obesity pose for society and what opportunities?

96 Alternative energy sources – According to BP and Royal Dutch Shell, it is likely that by 2050 up to one-third of the world's energy will need to come from alternative sources, i.e. solar, wind and other sources. Does this mean opportunities for innovation or facing a risk of scarcity?

97 An increasing middle class – China is likely to have over 45 million urban households by 2030 with annual incomes in excess of $70,000, putting it well ahead of Europe and closing the gap on North America. What opportunities and risks does an increasing middle class bring?

98 Standardization – the world has been becoming more standardized in areas such as transport (shipping containers), technology (computer operating systems) and business (accounting). Is this a risk or a benefit for the future?

99 Connectivity – The age of mobile phones for everyone is dawning, as Africa catches up on other parts of the world. More than 1 in 3 adults in Africa now has a mobile phone.

What risks and opportunities does this mean for the developing nations?

100 **Happiness** – Over 50 per cent of the world's population live in cities, which are typically built for function, efficiency and convenience. Should happiness be built into how they are planned for the future? Are we creating a risk for our society and well-being otherwise?

Notes and references

Chapter 1

Beck, U., *Risk Society: Towards a New Modernity* (London: Sage Publications, 1992)

US Nuclear Regulatory Commission:

http://www.nrc.gov/reading-rm/basic-ref/glossary/probabilistic-risk-assessment-pra.html

Hubbard, D., *The Failure of Risk Management: Why It's Broken and How to Fix It* (Hoboken: John Wiley & Sons, 2009), p. 46

Tversky, A. and Kahneman, D., 'Availability: A heuristic for judging frequency and probability', *Cognitive Psychology* (1973) 5(1): 207–33

Hald, A., *A History of Probability and Statistics and their Applications before 1750* (Hoboken: Wiley, 2003)

Bernstein, P., *Against the Gods: The Remarkable Story of Risk* (Hoboken: John Wiley & Sons, 1996)

'Mortality Statistics, Deaths Registered in England and Wales', Office For National Statistics 2009 (as reported in *The Guardian* 14 January 2011)

McNeill, W. H., *Plagues And Peoples* (Garden City, NY: Anchor Press, 1976)

http://www.theatlantic.com/technology/archive/2014/06/everything-we-know-about-facebooks-secret-mood-manipulation-experiment/373648/

Kramera, A., Guillory, J. and Hancock, J., 'Experimental evidence of massive-scale emotional contagion through social networks', *Proceedings of the National Academy of Sciences, USA* (2014) Vol 111, no. 24

Chapter 2

Pronovost, P., Needham, D., Berenholtz, S. *et al.* 'An Intervention to decrease catheter-related bloodstream infections in the ICU', *New England Journal of Medicine* (2006) 355: 2725–32

Kahneman, D. and Tversky, A. 'Prospect theory: An analysis of decision under risk', *Econometrica* (1979) 47(2), 263–91

Kahneman, D., *Thinking, Fast And Slow* (London: Penguin, 2011)

Blake, C., *The Art of Decisions* (London: Pearson Education, 2008)

Loewenstein, G., Weber, E., Hsee, C. and Welch, N., 'Risk as feelings', *Psychological Bulletin* (2001) Mar, 127(2): 267–86

Lerner, J. S. and Keltner, D., 'Toward a model of emotion-specific influences on judgement and choice', *Cognition and Emotion* (2000) 14(4): 473–93. doi: 10.1080/026999300402763

Reynolds, E. K., Schreiber, W. M., Geisel, K., MacPherson, L., Ernst, M. and Lejuez, C. W., 'Influence of social stress on risk-taking behavior in adolescents', *Journal of Anxiety Disorders* (Apr 2013) 27(3): 272–7

Gardner, D., *Risk: The Science and Politics of Fear* (London: Virgin, 2008)

www.patient.co.uk

Eysenck, M., Derakshan, N., Santos, R. and Calvo, M. G., 'Anxiety and cognitive performance: attentional control theory', *Emotion* (Washington DC, 2007) May, 7(2): 336–53)

Baumeister, R. F., Vohs, K. D. and Tice, D. M., 'The strength model of self-control', *Current Directions in Psychological Science* (2007) 16(6): 351–5. doi: 10.1111/j.1467-8721.2007.00534.x

Baker, T. B., Piper, M. E., McCarthy, D. E., Majeskie, M. R. and Fiore, M. C., 'Addiction motivation reformulated: An affective processing model of negative reinforcement', *Psychological Review* (2004) 111: 33–51. doi: 10.1037/0033-295X.111.1.33

Wildavsky, A. and Dake, K., 'Theories of risk perception: Who fears what and why?' *Daedalus* (1990) 19: 41–60

Beck, U., *Risk Society: Towards a New Modernity* (London: Sage Publications, 1992)

Anthony Giddens described a risk society as 'a society increasingly preoccupied with the future (and also with safety), which generates the notion of risk'.

Foucault, M., 'The Subject and Power', in Dreyfus, H., and Rabinow, P., *Michel Foucault: Beyond Structuralism and Hermeneutics* (Chicago: The University of Chicago Press, 1982), pp. 208–26

The Cultural Cognition Project at Yale Law School: www.culturalcognition.net/

The Invisible Gorilla: theinvisiblegorilla.com/videos.html

Trickey, G. and Stewart, M., 'Personality and risk tolerance', *The Risk-Type Compass Technical Manual*, (Tunbridge Wells: Psychological Consultancy Ltd, 2010)

McCrae, R. R. and Costa, P. T., 'Personality trait structure as a human universal', *American Psychologist* (1997) 52: 509–16

Chapter 3

www.baaa-acro.com/Liste%20des%20deces%20par%20annee.htm

Ellsberg, D., 'Risk, Ambiguity, And the Savage Axioms', *Quarterly Journal of Economics* (1961) 75(4): 643–69

Research study report, *The Role of Scientists in Public Debate* (Wellcome Trust, 2001)

Yates, N., *Beyond Evil* (London: John Blake Publishing, 2005)

Gill, T., *No Fear: Growing up in a risk-averse society* (London: Calouste Gulbenkian Foundation, 2007)

Green, H. and Hannon, C., *Their Space: Education for a Digital Generation* (London: Demos, 2007)

http://www.theriskfactory.org

World Development Report 2014, 'Risk and Opportunity: Managing Risk for Development': econ.worldbank.org

Rice, D. and Filippelli, G., 'One Cell Phone at a Time: Countering Corruption in Afghanistan', *Small Wars Journal* (2010)

White, D., 'The Social and Economic Impact of M-Pesa on the Lives of Women in the Fishing Industry on Lake Victoria', Independent Study Project (ISP) Collection (2012) Paper 1246

Grove, C. N., 'Introduction to the GLOBE Research Project on Leadership Worldwide' (2005): www.grovewell.com/pub-GLOBE-intro.html

Grove, C. N. 'Worldwide Differences in Business Values and Practices: Overview of GLOBE Research Findings' (2005): www.grovewell.com/pub-GLOBE-dimensions.html

http://geert-hofstede.com/dimensions.html

Casselman, B., 'Risk-averse culture infects US workers and entrepreneurs', *Wall Street Journal*, 2 June 2013: http://online.wsj.com/news/articles/SB10001424127887324031404578481162903760052

Robb, A., 'Far from the Wolf of Wall Street: how did young people become so risk averse?' *New Statesman*, 13 March 2014

Stangler, D., Ewing Marion Kauffman Foundation: http://online.wsj.com/news/articles/SB10001424127887324031404578481162903760052

Chapter 4
www.webershandwick.com The online research was conducted with KRC Research in October/November 2011 among 1,375 consumers and 575 senior executives in companies with annual revenues of $500 million or more. Respondents were located in four key markets: two developed markets (US and UK) and two emerging markets (China and Brazil).

http://www.bbc.co.uk/news/business-28370863

'Lance Armstrong dropped by three sponsors over doping evidence', BBC News, 18 October 2012: www.bbc.co.uk/sport/0/cycling/19978608

Murphy, J. E., 'Can The Scandals Teach Us Anything? Enron, Ethics and Lessons for Lawyers', *ABA Business Law Section* (American Bar Association, 2003) Vol 12, No. 3, January/February

Extract from BIS: Bank for International Settlements: http://www.bis.org/bcbs/

ONS: Office For National Statistics, National Life Tables, 2008–10: http://www.ons.gov.uk/ons/publications/re-reference-tables.html?edition=tcm%3A77-223324

Brent Spar Dossier – available from Shell: http://www-static.shell.com/content/dam/shell/static/gbr/downloads/e-and-p/brent-spar-dossier.pdf

Corporate Ecosystem Services Review, World Resources Institute *et al.*, 2008: www.waterfootprint.org/?page=files/home

Hoekstra, A. Y., Mekonnen, M. M., Chapagain, A. K., Mathews, R. E. and Richter, B. D., 'Global Monthly Water Scarcity: Blue Water Footprints versus Blue Water Availability' (2012) PLoS ONE 7(2): e32688. doi:10.1371/journal.pone.0032688

Climate Change 2013: *The Physical Science Basis*: http://www.climatechange2013.org/

Guidelines for Identifying Business Risks And Opportunities Arising from Ecosystem Change, Version 2.0 (WBCSD, Meridian Institute, 2012) The UK Cyber Security Strategy (The Cabinet Office, Nov 2011)

Chapter 5

Caspar Berry is a former professional poker player who is now a speaker and trainer catalysing change in some of the world's most successful companies: www.casparberry.com

'Traffic and Accident Data: Summary Statistics – Germany', Bundesanstalt für Straßenwesen (Federal Highway Research Institute)

The *Mary Rose* is a Tudor ship built in 1510, sunk in 1545 and rediscovered in 1971. Raised from the seabed in 1982, it is now housed in the Mary Rose Museum, Portsmouth, UK.

http://www.shell.com/global/future-energy/scenarios.html

http://www.brocku.ca/health-services/health-education/stress/eustress-distress

Chapter 6

World Economic Forum Global Risks report, 2014: www.weforum.org

Rapley, C. G., De Meyer, K., Carney, J., Clarke, R., Howarth, C., Smith, N., Stilgoe, J., Youngs, S., Brierley, C., Haugvaldstad, A., Lotto, B., Michie, S., Shipworth M. and Tuckett, D., 'Time for Change? Climate Science Reconsidered', Report of the UCL Policy Commission On Communicating Climate Science, 2014

Proceedings of the National Academy of Sciences (PNAS), 14 July 2014 111 (Supplement 3) 10860–67. doi:10.1073/pnas.1400817111

Corner, A., Whitmarsh, L. and Xenias, D., 'Uncertainty, scepticism and attitudes towards climate change: biased assimilation and attitude polarization', *Climatic Change* (2012) 114: 463–78

http://www.bbc.co.uk/news/health-28525974

Festinger, L., *A Theory of Cognitive Dissonance* (Stanford, CA: Stanford University Press, 1957)

'Communicating climate science' (House of Commons Science And Technology Committee, 2014)

'Global health risks: mortality and burden of disease attributable to selected major risks' (World Health Organization, 2009)

http://www.forbes.com/sites/parmyolson/2014/06/19/wearable-tech-health-insurance/

http://hetv.org/programmes/behaviour-change.htm

http://www.unilever.com/brands-in-action/detail/Lifebuoy/292086/

http://www.emarketer.com/Article/What-Health-Info-Do-Consumers-Seek-Online/1009698

http://www.ft.com/cms/s/0/a444e1f4-7f78-11e2-8d96-00144feabdc0.html#axzz385osYkpG

Steare, R., Stamboulides, P., Lewis, P.N., Plas, L., Wilton, P. and Woodman, P., *Managers and their Moral DNA* (Chartered Management Institute, March 2014)

https://www.youtube.com/watch?v=MLxFwZXTfks

Heffernan, M., *Wilful Blindness* (London: Simon & Schuster, 2012)

100 ideas

http://www.nsc.org/NSC%20Picture%20Library/News/web_graphics/Injury_Facts_37.pdf

http://www.discovery.com/tv-shows/curiosity/topics/big-question-what-are-odds-of-surviving-plane-crash.htm

http://www.twinsuk.co.uk/twinstips/18/189/multiple-birth-statistics-facts-and-trivia/what-are-the-chances-of-having-twinstriplets-or-quads-/

http://www.theguardian.com/news/datablog/2011/aug/04/live-to-100-likely

http://www.who.int/whr/2003/chapter1/en/index2.html

http://www.funny2.com/odds.htm

http://www.wired.co.uk/magazine/archive/2014/01/features/the-winning-formula

http://www.sheknows.com/living/articles/1023453/what-are-the-odds-21-statistics-that-will-surprise-you

Danaei, G., Ding, E. L., Mozaffarian D. *et al.*, 'The preventable causes of death in the United States: comparative risk assessment of dietary, lifestyle, and metabolic risk factors' PLoS Med. 2009; 6:e1000058

Oxford Economics, *Global Cities 2030*: http://www.oxfordeconomics.com/cities/report

ALL THAT MATTERS: RISK

Index

All That Matters books are written by the world's leading experts, to introduce the most exciting and relevant areas of an important topic to students and general readers.

From Bioethics to Muhammad and Philosophy to Sustainability, the *All That Matters* series covers the most controversial and engaging topics from science, philosophy, history, religion and other fields. The authors are world-class academics or top public intellectuals, on a mission to bring the most interesting and challenging areas of their subject to new readers.

Each book contains a unique '100 ideas' section, giving inspiration to readers whose interest has been piqued and who want to explore the subject further. Find out more, at: www.allthatmattersbooks.com
Facebook/allthatmattersbooks
Twitter@All_That_Matters